PRAISE FOR
THE ACCIDENTAL MARKETER

"As a formally-trained veterinarian that found myself in a marketing role, I truly am an 'Accidental Marketer'! I have personally used the tools in this book to successfully lead the launch and rebranding of several products—as if I have been a marketer my entire career."

—Shelley Stanford
Director, Technical Services, Zoetis

"I have been waiting for you to write this book! Given my experiences over the years with you, I can't think of a better approach to help businesses succeed!"

—Lesley Fronio
Worldwide Vice President, Commercial Marketing,
Ortho Clinical Diagnostics

"As a founder of Impact Planning Group over 35 years ago, I am proud to see that these tools have been time-tested with thousands of companies, and continue to add value to organizations and their customers."

—James Mac Hulbert, R. C.
Kopf Professor Emeritus,
Columbia University and Visiting Professor,
Guanghua School of Management, Peking University

"As an Accidental Marketer who was trained as a chemist, I have learned to love the discipline of this type of approach to marketing. Tom and Mary make applying process and tools both fun and highly productive."

—Lynn Rosen
Global Director Special Formulas;
Opinion Leader and Advocacy LEAD
at Wyeth Nutrition, a part of Nestle SA

"Shackleton's famous recruitment ad in the *Times of London* with the headline, 'Men Wanted for Hazardous Journey' is how an inexperienced marketer might feel. Believe me, *The Accidental Marketer* is an essential survival kit for those courageous enough to venture into marketing's uncharted waters!"

—Bryan Mattimore
Author, *Idea Stormers*;
President of The Growth Engine Company

The
Accidental
Marketer

POWER TOOLS

for People Who Find Themselves in

MARKETING ROLES

TOM SPITALE
MARY ABBAZIA

WILEY

Cover image: White Flash ©iStockphoto/MihailUlianikov
Cover design: Wiley

Published by John Wiley & Sons, Inc., Hoboken, New Jersey.
Published simultaneously in Canada.

For general information about our other products and services, please contact our Customer Care Department within the United States at (800) 762-2974, outside the United States at (317) 572-3993 or fax (317) 572-4002.

Wiley publishes in a variety of print and electronic formats and by print-on-demand. Some material included with standard print versions of this book may not be included in e-books or in print-on-demand. If this book refers to media such as a CD or DVD that is not included in the version you purchased, you may download this material at http://booksupport.wiley.com. For more information about Wiley products, visit www.wiley.com.

ISBN: 978-1-118-79741-9 (cloth)
ISBN: 978-1-118-79739-6 (ebk)
ISBN: 978-1-118-79743-3 (ebk)

Printed in the United States of America
10 9 8 7 6 5 4 3 2 1

The
Accidental
Marketer

*This book is dedicated to my wife, Dawn, whose love
and devotion makes all things possible, and to my
children, Sarah, Thomas, and Gianni, who have inspired
me more than they will ever know.*
—Tom

*I am dedicating this book to my incredible husband, Tim, who
constantly encourages me to try new things, and to my children,
T.J. and Sophia, who make life so interesting and fun.*
—Mary

Contents

Preface

ARE YOU AN ACCIDENTAL MARKETER?

It's happening with even the most straightforward products all around you: doorknobs with microchips to recognize a homeowner instead of locks, wooden pallets with microprocessors that wholesalers use to load merchandise in the exact order each retailer stocks it, an emerging Internet of things where virtually every product comes with a Web-connected chip that collects information and makes it smart.

With technology being built into goods of all kinds, we are finding more and more businesses hiring or transferring in scientists and engineers to fulfill marketing roles.

This new world creates a challenge for businesses. Finding and nurturing marketing strategy leaders has never been more conflicting. Certainly, hiring people who have technical depth *and* a strategic marketing background would be nirvana. But it's rare to find this combination of skills.

Instead, businesses struggle with the trade-off of having a marketing team with deep technical knowledge and limited marketing skills and experience or vice versa. And as technology progresses, more companies are erring on the side of technical knowledge.

We refer to these companies as Business Scientists, meaning that they have engineers, scientists, or other technically minded professionals serving in business and marketing roles. And we call the people who are actually serving in these marketing roles Accidental Marketers. Does this describe you or someone you know?

We have also learned that not all Accidental Marketers work in large, Business Scientist organizations. Many entrepreneurs, small-business managers, and fund-raisers face the challenges of marketing without marketing-specific education or backgrounds. They are Accidental Marketers, too.

Whatever path you took to unexpectedly find yourself in a marketing role, this book is for you. We were inspired to write it so that more people can benefit from the type of content and tools we use in our live workshops. These in-person sessions help Accidental Marketers from some of the worlds' largest, most recognizable companies succeed.

WHAT ABOUT EXPERIENCED MARKETERS?

"So what did you think?" Tom nervously asked Joao, the newly appointed regional Chief Marketing Officer for a global industrial company. We were nearing the end of a workshop, and Joao's product marketing managers had just spent three days creating new marketing plans using our tools and frameworks.

We were nervous because Joao had just come to the industrial company from a well-known consumer products company. Like many of his former colleagues, he had an MBA and experience managing a big portfolio of recognizable consumer brands.

"I loved it," he said. "We used some marketing frameworks and tools at my previous company, but nothing as comprehensive and interconnected as what I just saw from your approach."

We were thrilled, of course, but also surprised. We'd assumed that our type of content and approach would be the standard in leading consumer products companies. But we have since learned that's not always the case.

Not all the marketers in our workshops are inexperienced; seasoned marketers also find new ideas and fresh approaches. They too discover that our tools are useful for aligning their team and communicating their plans to team members and executives that are not experienced marketers.

HOW THIS BOOK CAN HELP ACCIDENTAL MARKETERS

"What else have you tried?" we asked a prospective new client interviewing our firm. She managed a team of intelligent and technically adept individuals who lacked marketing experience. They needed help developing skills and tools to create strategies and value propositions that maximized the market share of her firm's products.

"We've had guest lectures from authors and professors, fascinating case studies. But always we're left with translating the lessons to our business on our own, and it hasn't led to much change."

We hear this all the time. Understanding the *stories* of how the best companies succeeded is an important aspect of improving marketing strategies. We'll share many such cases in this book.

But significant improvement in strategies happens when these stories are *translated* into tools that can be used immediately and applied to *any* business. That's what our firm does—we reverse-engineer marketing's greatest successes into frameworks that help even inexperienced marketers rapidly learn how to *differentiate* their products and services.

Our unique perspectives on the stories about familiar names and oft-cited brands are a by-product of our company's 35-year quest to understand, specifically, what drives marketing success. The accompanying tools are a result of our passionate mission: to enable companies with nontraditional marketers to understand these principles and immediately build a new, improved, differentiated marketing plan in the span of a two- to three-day workshop.

Our company has taught this approach mainly to major organizations via live, private strategy sessions, as well as to executives attending the workshops we conduct at Columbia University and California's Institute of Technology (Caltech). This book allows us to reach a wider audience with practical and profitable information.

WHY THIS BOOK IS *EVEN MORE* APPLICABLE TO BUSINESS-TO-BUSINESS ACCIDENTAL MARKETERS

A majority of our clients are in business-to-business (B2B) markets, in industries ranging from power generation to oil and gas services, to drug pharmaceuticals sold to specialist physicians. Because B2B products and services are often more technical in nature, a higher percentage of Accidental Marketers are in these types of industries.

So why, you might ask after looking at the table of contents, are there so many business-to-consumer (B2C) companies featured in the book?

In our experience, there aren't many, for instance, power generation marketing success stories floating around. And although most successful marketers tend to prefer to keep their winning formulas private, it's much more difficult to hide a B2C success.

When we reverse-engineer great marketing, our goal is to study cases with which B2B marketers are familiar and make tools that apply in their marketing situations. Rest assured, there are plenty of B2B cases in this book. But often we find that it's our clients' *personal* experiences with the products from companies like Apple, Enterprise, Southwest, and Dell that allow them to translate important lessons to their own B2B markets.

So even though B2B industries tend to be more complex, with more varied stakeholders, customers who are often purchasing agents or other professionals instead of consumers, and so on, our tools are designed to specifically work in these situations.

How to Use This Book

The Accidental Marketer was written to follow the approach of our company's in-person strategy sessions. We are constantly challenged during these live workshops to hold the attention of highly demanding businesspeople over several days. Therefore, our case studies have to be entertaining and relevant, with information participants likely haven't heard before. And because the clock is always ticking, the tools we use must be immediately applicable and actionable.

We wrote this book with these same principles in mind. Not only does each chapter provide fresh perspective on a company's success, it also gives the recipe for duplicating the strategy uniquely in *your* industry. That is because the last section of each chapter features one of Impact's power tools, with full instructions and, usually, an additional helpful example.

In addition, you'll see that the flow of the following 10 chapters of *The Accidental Marketer* follow the design of a great marketing plan, an approach we call outside-in. *Outside* marketing factors refer to strategy components that are important to address but typically beyond what a company can control—things such as economic trends, customer needs, and competitors. *Inside* factors, conversely, are defined as the unique, core capabilities that a company currently has or can easily develop or acquire. The optimal strategy combines both concepts in the proper order.

The chapters begin with cases and tools that will help you understand and develop world-class situation assessments and strategies (Chapters 1–3). The middle chapters encapsulate the elements of competitive analysis and internal core competency assessment (Chapters 4–7). The later chapters bring the analyses together to create world-class offerings that set companies apart (Chapters 8–10).

If you don't have the time to read the entire book sequentially, you may want to visit our website at www.theaccidentalmarketer.com. There you will find an assessment that will help diagnose which chapters are most relevant to your situation, along with other valuable bonus content.

Although all the tools are interconnected, most of the chapters can largely stand on their own and provide you with some immediate help. If you are in a hurry, you may want to jump right to the tools sections that you find most critical.

HAVE FUN AND ENJOY YOURSELF—YOU JUST MIGHT FIND YOU HAVE A PASSION FOR MARKETING

However you choose to navigate through this book, we hope you will do so with an open mind, a commitment to excellence, and a light heart. In our opinion, marketing strategy is the most enjoyable aspect of business. Every one of our workshop sessions is accompanied by much fun, laughter, and enthusiastic conversation. The creative juices are flowing, and minds are being opened. Industry-changing ideas—many of which are featured in this book—come out of this type of environment.

In addition to the fun, we often find that the process of using our tools ignites passion for their new role in the hearts of Accidental Marketers. This makes us very happy, as being able to enjoy one's work is one of the greatest blessings in life.

We have been fortunate to spend more than a decade doing work we are passionate about. It's satisfying to be a part of a business where many successful ideas are launched and careers advanced.

That's why we are extremely excited to bring our content to you and a wider audience. We trust that you'll see our passion for marketing come through in the ensuing pages and hope you enjoy the book as much as we have loved writing it!

Tom Spitale
Mary Abbazia

Acknowledgments

A book like this is possible only through our interaction with literally thousands of clients and colleagues. We are so appreciative of the contributions of everyone we've had the pleasure to work with over the years. It is impossible to acknowledge here everyone who deserves to be mentioned, but special thanks are due to the following people:

Thanks to the fantastic team at our publisher, John Wiley & Sons, Inc.: Brian Neill, Christine Moore, Charlotte Maiorana, Peter Knox, Susan Moran, and the production team.

Special acknowledgment goes to our European partner at Impact, Sean Welham, for going far above and beyond the call of duty. Sean is the type of guy who can do anything with excellence. Not only did he contribute his brilliance to many of the cases and other content in the book, he showed that he can use both sides of his brain in serving as our de facto art director for the book.

Thanks to our amazing Impact team who makes work fun, including Mel Ingold, Paul DiPrato, Debby Pratt, Rob Hoctor, Martin Ma, Randy Boytos, Lisa Dazzo, and John Tiburzi.

To Tom's incredible sister, Angela Begert, who is also our travel coordinator, proofreader, and manager of thousands of details. Thanks for your infinite patience and willingness to work across all time zones when we are on the road—which is most of the time!

Thanks to Impact's founders, the people who have shaped the tools and concepts through the start of Impact Planning Group, the late Dr. William Brandt, Professor James (Mac) Hulbert, and Robert Christian.

Thanks also to our creative partners, Carolyn Walker and her Response Marketing team, including Cosmo Iannopollo, Terry Lush, and Corey Petrini, who helped us greatly on the charts and tables in this book.

The following people have made incredible contributions to our thinking—and to the world of marketing: Jay Moore from GE; Tom Niehaus of Niehaus Enterprises; Bruno Bert and Lynn Rosen of Wyeth Nutrition; Bob Baker at Pfizer; Don Peppers, Martha Rogers, and Marji Chimes from Peppers and Rogers Group.

We would also like to give special thanks to the following people who helped us further enhance our stories and tools: At Bloomberg Tradebook, Liron Mandelbaum, Rick Gould; California Institute of Technology, Anne Campbell; Ciba and Syngenta, Nicola Lelli, Rob Neill; Columbia University, Professor Michel Pham, Ethan Hanabury, Professor Noel Capon; Convatec, Margo Skinner; Covidien, Scott Herring, Bryan Hanson, Tim Nolan, Chris Barry, Ralph Corradi, Kerr Holbrook, Chris Ward; FuelCell Energy, Bruce Ludemann; General Electric, especially Beth Comstock, Nancy Martin, Darryl Dougan, Rich Braaten, Fred Virgin, Raghu Krishnamoorthy, Dan Henson, Elizabeth Sena, Viv Goldstein, Doug Scott, Ralph Elwell, Bob Lobly; J&J, Lesley Fronio, Alyson Wess, Lynn Hall, Jonathan Meek, Marti Heckman, Leigh Ann Soltysiak; Netafim, Michael Dowgert, Diane Noecker; Praxair, Marcos Perello; Pfizer, Jillian O'Neill, Albert Bourla, Susan O'Connor, Marina Gertsek, Ilya Belenkiy, Alyson Lehanski, Anna Kotis, Radife Kiral, Jim Maffezoli; Prudential Financial, Gaurang Pandya; Takeda Pharmaceuticals, Michael Williams, Rene Gilvert; Terumo BCT, Lisa Hayes, Teri Motheral; United Technologies Corporation, Scott Wiley, Linda Scott; Wyeth Nutrition, Mickey Lee, Nell D'Auria, Mike Russomano; Zoetis, Alejandro Bernal, Gloria Basse, Johan Dreesen, Jon Lowe, Jolian Howell, Julie Baker, Shelley Stanford, Alvaro Aldaz, Pablo Lamberto; as well as other special friends whom we have worked with, including Mel Schatz, Steve Sitek, Dan Carrothers, Trish Watson, and Jaki Sitterle.

We'd also want to express our sincere gratitude to several people who helped us get the book off the ground: Bryan Mattimore, Trini and H.P. Newquist, Carrie O'Donnell, and Frank Mari.

And special thanks to the man who helped the authors and John Wiley & Sons, Inc., find each other—Mike Barlow. We hope you enjoyed the bottle of champagne, Mike!

CHAPTER 1

Who Moved
My . . . Customer?

The Simple Concept behind Dell's Success in the PC Market

POWER TOOL: INFLUENCER MAP

I don't skate to where the puck is; I skate to where the puck is going to be.
—Wayne Gretzky, aka "The Great One," one
of the greatest hockey players of all time

A TOOL TO DETECT SHIFTS IN DECISION-MAKING POWER BEFORE YOUR COMPETITORS DO

"Are you sure you want to start the book with a story about Dell?" one of our advisors asked with a raised eyebrow. A very successful business author himself, our coach was voicing a legitimate concern about the overexposed nature of some case histories, especially stories about companies whose star has somewhat faded.

But we convinced him that the Dell story is a great way to start off the book. And we'll use the same argument to persuade you to pay close attention to this chapter.

With regard to the faded star nature of Dell's current business, wouldn't any business like to have a 20-year run like Dell did from 1984 to 2004, when the company grew from a founder's dorm room to the number one position in the massive personal computers industry? Any lessons gleaned from Dell's meteoric rise are worth learning if they can deliver even a fraction of this kind of growth.

Although many business professionals, including Accidental Marketers, have heard Dell's story, only a few have made any significant changes to their own business strategy *based on it*. We can confidently say, after conducting hundreds of workshops, that virtually *every* client we work with *improves* their strategy based on the Dell case as we present it.

We know this because we *translate* Dell's strategies (and a few other mini-cases in the chapter) into a tool—one that helps you immediately apply Dell's lessons in your industry. We'll provide important, interesting background facts about Dell's marketing approach, but the tool—called an Influencer Map—will allow you to make a key *decision* that will drive the rest of your customer-focused marketing strategy.

Influencer Maps show Accidental Marketers how to detect shifts in customer and stakeholder decision-making power in a market before their competitors do. Of the 10 tools that make up our base set, Influencer Maps are one of the most popular with our clients. Once you see how simple yet powerful they can be, you will share their enthusiasm!

THE ROOTS OF AN INDUSTRY REVOLUTION

At the very beginnings of the personal computer era back in 1984, Michael Dell realized he had some seemingly unrelated skills. He'd already had several successful direct mail ventures in junior high school and high school. Selling stamps and trading cards had netted him $2,000 in profits at the ripe old age of 12. A few years later, he utilized a mailing list of newly married couples to sell newspaper subscriptions. He made enough money to buy himself a BMW while still in high school.

As a freshman at the University of Texas, Dell had figured out how to take apart and put back together an IBM personal computer (PC).

He started a successful computer upgrade business that he ran out of his dorm room, which allowed him to deeply understand the economics of computer selling.

The combination of Michael Dell's computer prowess and direct mail experiences was about to create an opportunity that would revolutionize the industry. And the simple concept behind that opportunity hadn't even occurred to the big PC manufacturers of the time.

THE BIG GUYS GET BLINDED BY THE CUSTOMER STATUS QUO

As Michael Dell contemplated a new type of PC business, strategic planners for the leading manufacturers of the time, such as IBM, Compaq, and Tandy, were likely preoccupied with product-oriented issues. Because computer use grew by more than 750 percent from 1980 to 1985, merely being able to predict and supply this exploding demand was a constant, focus-sapping concern for the market leaders.

Another element that distracted PC strategists was the implications of Moore's Law. This amazingly accurate theory, postulated by Gordon Moore, the founder of computer chip giant, Intel, predicted that computing power would double every 18 months. This geometric progression of chip technology led to a dizzying pace of new PC features and functions, which all competitors were struggling to keep up with.

At least one element of the industry that *seemed* stable was the method for distributing and selling PCs. Computers reached consumers via distributors, value-added resellers and retailer networks that each big manufacturer had painstakingly built. The process worked this way because computers were considered a highly technical item requiring expert hand-holding and assistance during the decision-making process.

A simple diagram shows how the era's leading manufacturers likely viewed decision-making power in the PC market at the time. Each circle in Figure 1.1 represents a stakeholder. The size of the circle indicates decision-making power, with the arrows indicating how each stakeholder influences the others in the chain.

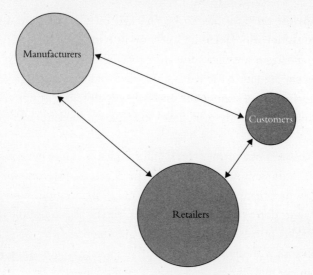

Figure 1.1   Decision-Making Power in the 1980s Personal Computer Market: Likely View of the Leading Manufacturers

Source: Copyright © 2014 Impact Planning Group. All rights reserved.

Although Figure 1.1 may have been technically correct, it doesn't account for how the decision-making power of each of these stakeholders was *changing* in a very dynamic market. Judging by their actions, Dell's competitors likely assumed that the power structure in the market would remain relatively consistent. In fact, they acted as if they believed that only computer nerds and scientists would be comfortable making decisions about which PC to buy without expert assistance. This would prove to be a dangerous—and eventually fatal—competitive assumption that Dell Inc. took full advantage of.

YOU CAN ASSESS CHANGING INFLUENCE NOW—OR RISK LOSING TO A COMPETITOR WHO DOES

It's at precisely this time in a market—things are going well, sales are growing, the industry is in an early life cycle phase—when companies tend to focus extremely closely on product. Even suggesting that a company reassess its customer/stakeholder chain is often considered a throwaway strategic step.

Organizations see this as a box to be checked on the way to out-product-featuring the competition, focusing solely on its traditional customers.

But time and again, we find companies that are doing one of two very different things: they're either capitalizing on stakeholder power shifts or finding themselves locked *out* of strong relationships with customer groups that faster-thinking competitors already own. Some examples of the latter are:

- The marketers of a former blockbuster drug, now off-patent, who put all of their resources toward selling to general practitioners and specialists—and now find themselves late to the game in figuring out how to ensure pharmacists don't switch customers to a generic version of the drug
- The makers of baby formulas in emerging markets who don't have any relationships with their country's governmental policy-makers—until the government pulls the product from all retail shelves based on a perceived health issue that turns out to be unwarranted
- The manufacturers of a technically superior hip implant who have forgotten to call on managers of a key administrative hospital function—the operating room scheduler, who then promoted a competitor's inferior product because they didn't understand the more advanced device's benefits and because they thought the implanting operation took too long

On the positive side, we see companies achieving tremendous growth by anticipating stakeholder shifts. Network management software company SolarWinds has developed a product positioned as a low-priced solution sold directly to information technology (IT) managers rather than chief information officers (CIOs).

SolarWinds correctly anticipated a corporate trend that is pushing certain IT decisions downward in organizations. The industry moved from an environment in which CIOs made virtually all software decisions to one in which companies trust IT managers to make certain decisions within defined budgetary guidelines.

SolarWinds capitalized on this trend by focusing its marketing resources to understand and serve company network managers' particular and specific needs. The resulting customized value proposition—a software subscription price that fits a typical IT manager's budget, a direct selling model that efficiently replaces face-to-face sales, immediate download of the product upon purchase, a thriving business-to-business social network of IT manager peers dedicated to helping each other with network management issues—has led to tremendous growth. SolarWinds is averaging 25 percent quarterly earnings and sales growth over the past year.

Remember these ideas—recognizing shifts in stakeholder power and tailoring value propositions to these unique stakeholders' needs—as we return to our Dell story.

DELL CAPITALIZES ON A POWER SHIFT

If you spoke to him in 1984, Michael Dell might tell you that he would have been happy to dominate the early adopter PC market. Or maybe, he would say that he'd planned to dominate the entire PC industry from the outset.

In either event, he made the decision to sell PCs via mail order *directly to consumers,* an approach that was successful immediately. When gross monthly revenues reached $80,000, Michael dropped out of college and focused on his venture full-time. The growth of this direct marketing–focused strategy was undeniable—$6 million in its first full year of business, $40 million the next, with continued rapid leaps forward in sales for the foreseeable future.

Could *all* of this business be coming from nerds and scientists? Or was it possible that Dell had recognized a fundamental shift in decision-making power, one that was rendering more mainstream consumers confident in their ability to buy a computer directly from a manufacturer?

DELL TESTS THE RETAIL CHANNEL BUT PULLS BACK

As the 1980s rolled along, the dominant PC manufacturers continued to invest heavily in retail spiffs, commissions, and a bloated structure that added cost. And Dell also hedged its channel bets in the early days.

Some new executives who had come over from competitor Tandy convinced Michael to build a Dell version of a traditional retail organization in 1987. This group would expand Dell's distribution by selling the company's PCs via stores.

However, Michael soon grew impatient with the experiment, which was proved to deliver drastically reduced margins for his organization. Although the (soon-to-be-fired-or-quit) former Tandy executives would probably argue that the distribution initiative didn't have enough time to deliver acceptable returns, Michael felt he had enough evidence that direct marketing was the way to go. And he did: the company had sales of $157 million in 1987, mostly via direct channels, at very healthy margins.

DELL'S PREPARATION MEETS A HUGE OPPORTUNITY: BEYOND NERDS AND SCIENTISTS

Dell's sales in 1987 were all the evidence the company needed that a profound power shift in PC industry influence was indeed occurring. It was clear that it was not just nerds and scientists who were comfortable buying computers directly.

The Moore's Law–driven industry was quickly making PCs that were easier and easier to use. Therefore, the typical consumer was becoming increasingly confident in making this technical purchase directly. The value-add of the traditional distribution channel was becoming less significant—very quickly.

This was the time for Dell to move even more boldly. Dell's direct contact with its customers was a distinct advantage over the big manufacturers, whose only diluted access to customers was through their distribution channel. Because the channel believed they *owned* the customer relationships, they didn't allow much direct contact: they were afraid of being cut out of a lucrative distribution loop.

Dell took advantage of its direct customer access to better understand—and more important, *predict*—exactly what those customers wanted. This contributed strongly to its now-famous model of building computers only *after* the customer's order was in hand. Compare this with competitors that manufactured PCs sold by independent retail distributors. They had to predict retail demand from an arms-length standpoint and guess how many computers to make.

As Dell continued to build its direct marketing infrastructure and revolutionary operational strategy, it began to realize some significant competitive advantages. And then, something fortuitous happened.

There's a famous saying that luck is the intersection of preparation and opportunity. The growth of the Internet in the 1990s was the opportunity that perfectly intersected with Dell's preparation in creating a world-class direct-selling infrastructure. The company that had a dominant PC-direct computer-selling model was a perfect match for the world's newest, best-ever direct-selling channel: the World Wide Web.

DELL.COM COMPLETES THE DAVID VERSUS GOLIATH STORY

When it debuted in 1996, Dell.com enabled a whole new level of direct marketing efficiencies. It integrated its customer order system with its suppliers, enabling further value chain efficiencies. Customers could browse, configure, and track computer orders online, without help (unless they wanted it), adding further margins to the business in reduced customer service costs. Website "click" data further enhanced Dell's ability to keep its finger on the pulse of customer needs.

With Dell.com providing a huge platform, Dell claimed the top spot in PC sales in 2001. This completed a less-than-20-year journey that began in a college dorm room and culminated in the company rising to the top of a huge, growing industry. In 2004, Michael Dell announced that he was stepping down as CEO, a move that he has reversed and rereversed several times over the past 9 years. There is little doubt that this back-and-forth is at least partially responsible for some of the tough times the company has faced since then.

THE SIMPLE SECRET TO DELL'S MARKETING SUCCESS

To really understand Dell's success, we need to look beyond Dell's innovative supply chain model and its good fortune to be a direct-selling expert at the advent of the Internet. That's where we find a fundamental secret essential to revolutionizing many industries—or less dramatically (but still important) unlocking success in an underperforming product or portfolio.

Dell first had to define its customer priorities by understanding not just where stakeholder power rests today but how that power is shifting and changing.

Redrawing Figure 1.1 by making one small change shows how Dell likely viewed the market. Adding a dotted circle to show how each stakeholder's influence in the market is *changing* is a most important piece of information in a dynamic market (Figure 1.2). And today, almost all markets are dynamic!

While other manufacturers focused on product issues, Dell capitalized on a huge power shift in the market. Specifically, it placed a bet on the growing confidence of consumers in purchasing PCs directly from Dell. Other manufacturers missed this shift and kept focusing on selling almost exclusively through retailers. Like the quote from the great Gretzky at the opening of this chapter, Dell skated to where the puck was going.

Without this fundamental analysis and decision, Dell would have probably ended up as a commodity-like, price-based, apples-to-apples competitor of IBM and the like. Deciding who *a company's priority stakeholders are*—essentially, defining a company's most important customer—is an early step to a world-class strategy. That's why this topic of stakeholder influence is the first chapter of this book.

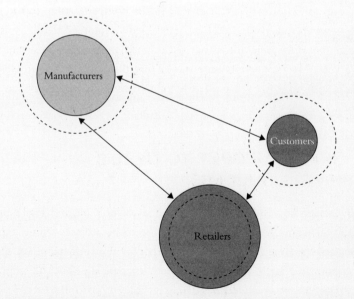

Figure 1.2   Decision-Making Power in the 1980s Personal Computer Market: Likely View of Dell

Source: Copyright © 2014 Impact Planning Group. All rights reserved.

This type of analysis lets companies make decisions on how to spend their marketing resources on various stakeholders in order to understand them, create offerings for them, and sell to them. But how can companies do this effectively, especially when it comes to determining how stakeholder power is shifting?

DUPLICATING DELL'S STAKEHOLDER INSIGHTS UNIQUELY IN YOUR INDUSTRY: INFLUENCER MAPPING

Figure 1.2, which shows how Dell viewed the market, is an example of an Influencer Map, a framework we've developed over the past 35 years. It's a resource allocation tool that you can use to create an early decision point in a world-class marketing strategy. It diagrams current and changing influences in an industry. It is an important tool for a marketing plan. The following describes how you can create an Influencer Map for your organization.

Step 1: The first step in building an Influencer Map is to make an exhaustive list of *everyone* in an industry who can influence the choice of purchasing your type of product or service. This is not easy, mainly because this list should include even nonbuyers who nonetheless affect decisions, such as industry consultants, academics, and influential Web bloggers.

This first step's unbreakable rule is, "Don't miss anybody." The aforementioned hip implant company suffered needlessly for years with a poor performing, technically superior product when they violated this rule and missed an important stakeholder: the operating room scheduler.

Step 2: The next step is to then assign small, medium, or large solid-line circles to indicate each stakeholder's current level of decision-making power. Then, draw dotted-line circles to show *how influence is changing* for each stakeholder. If the dotted circle is inside the solid circle, then that stakeholder's decision-making influence is *shrinking*. Dotted circles outside the solid line indicate *growing* influence. And no dotted circle means no change is occurring.

Step 3: Next, add arrows to indicate how each stakeholder *influences other* stakeholders; sometimes this influence is light (dotted arrows). The influence often works bidirectionally, with each stakeholder influencing the other; this is indicated by double-tipped arrows. Sometimes, the influence goes in only one direction (single-tipped arrows).

Step 4: Once the map is drawn, the real work begins: determining resource decisions based on the map. You do this by asking two analysis questions: Who were the top three stakeholders, in terms of allocating marketing and sales time and effort *prior to this analysis?* Then, how should our priorities change, *based on the Influencer Map?*

HOW INFLUENCER MAPS CAN HELP YOU MAKE STRATEGY-CHANGING DECISIONS—LIKE THIS INFANT FORMULA COMPANY DID

The results of this strategic process can be as profound as uncovering industry-changing approaches like Dell's. But less dramatic discoveries are frequently unearthed as well. Influencer Maps always shape strategies in a significant way, as the explanation of the map that follows will illustrate. This particular example shows industry power in a retail and health care environment. The product is infant formula, the powder substance that becomes milk-like, an alternative to breast milk, when water is added.

We worked with this global client several years ago when it was trying to reach a $1 billion revenue goal. Margins were getting *squeezed* by the retailer customers who didn't see the incremental value in the high-quality ingredients, processing, and support that our client provided.

We guided the company through the key questions of "Who influences the market now?" and "Who will be driving the decisions in the future?" They created the Influencer Map shown in Figure 1.3.

Prior to drawing the map, our client's priorities had been to spend the vast majority of its resources calling on retailers, medical professionals,

(continued)

(*continued*)

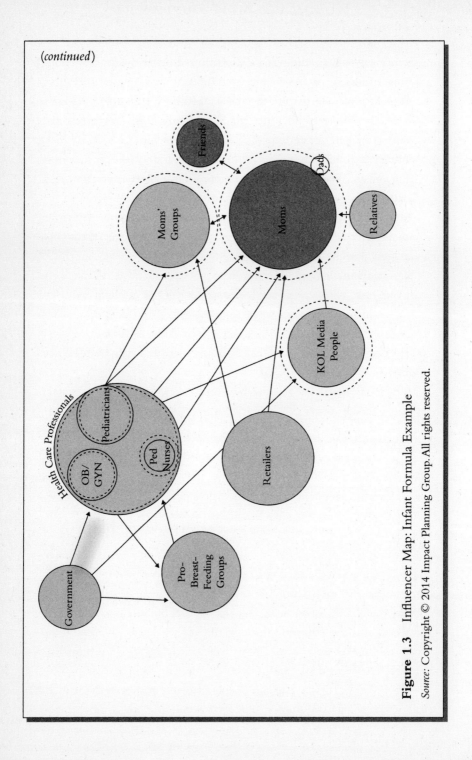

Figure 1.3 Influencer Map: Infant Formula Example

and hospital staff. In the future, management realized that they would still need to focus on the medical professionals and hospital staff; however, they could clearly see that they needed to shift some resources from retailers to developing loyalty by communicating directly to moms (where and when statutes allowed).

Their dilemma was that they had very little consumer expertise. Making matters more difficult, breast-feeding statutes kept them from embarking on many types of typical direct-to-consumer strategies.

It took them several years to develop the appropriate expertise and strategies. But as they shifted their priorities and resources, their company grew past the $1 billion mark . . . to $2 billion.

The Influencer Map allows you to have the kind of strategy discussions that can change the fortune of products, portfolios, and entire companies. When you gather cross-functional industry experts from inside—and, if possible, *outside*—your company for this discussion, you enhance your chances of drawing an accurate map of your industry.

Influencer Maps are technically correct when they represent your industry expert team's best judgment. Typically, a few reasonably short sessions with your team will provide enough information to develop confidence that the map approximates the actual market situation. If you need to quickly verify the map, ask some of your stakeholders, "What were the last three things that you purchased?" and "What was your role in those decisions?" This should give you a better indication of their actual decision-making or influencing power. You can also show your customers the map and ask them to help you refine it.

We'd led hundreds of Influencer Map discussions—and we can confidently say that if your priorities after building the map are the same as your priorities before you built the map, your map is wrong! Industries are changing too fast, and inertia in companies is too strong, for us to accept that a company has its current marketing and sales resources exactly aligned. Our typical response to this status quo finding is to dig deeper.

(*continued*)

(continued)

BUILDING ON INFLUENCER MAPS TO UNDERSTAND STAKEHOLDER NEEDS

Influencer Maps help you identify "Who moved my customer?" . . . and how you might move your customer. Although these maps are a key, early step to a brilliant, customer-centric marketing strategy, there are other important things to do as well. Once you've uncovered a priority stakeholder group, it is essential to understand—better than any other competitor in the stakeholder's consideration set—what the customer's needs are. That is the subject of our next chapter.

CHAPTER 2

The Fountain from Which Great Marketing Flows

How Holiday Inn Express Inspired Price-Conscious Travelers to Pay More and Other Stories of Insight

POWER TOOL: THE BENEFITS LADDER

> *Only when inspired to go beyond consciousness by some extraordinary insight does beauty manifest unexpectedly.*
>
> —Arthur Erickson, famous Canadian architect

TURNING DATA INTO INSIGHT REQUIRES SKILL AND PERSISTENCE

As a society, we are ambivalent about very inquisitive children who constantly ask "Why?" A current popular car commercial illustrates this outlook well. It features a man doing chores outside his home. He's nervously trying to avoid the precocious neighbor kid while, at the same time, marveling at how the child's constant inquisition made him think deeply about the decisions he's made.

This uncertainty toward inquisition might help explain an odd phenomenon we observe among many of our consulting clients. They place more emphasis than ever on gathering data and getting close to the customer, but their inquiries and analysis always seem to stop a bit short of turning the information they gather into the types of discoveries that drive innovation, sales, and profits.

Maybe marketers are worried about annoying customers by asking "Why?" just one more time. They fail to realize that they may be just one well-articulated question away from unlocking a new discovery that can create tremendous value for their customers and their business.

In studying our clients' and competitors' marketing strategies, we see how virtually every company in a market thinks they already know the full range of what customers want. How can we tell? The various approaches all seem to address the same handful of needs that these brands have *assumed* are the hot buttons of every industry customer (e.g., convenience, reliability, safety, durability, efficacy).

But without developing any *new* understanding of customer needs, business creativity comes to a standstill. Assuming that every notion of customer needs has been uncovered, marketers get frustrated and stagnant. They start believing that they've already tried every idea of how to serve customers.

It's difficult for customers as well. They feel like all the providers are selling the same thing they always have and are simply trying to outshout each other. They see no difference in value propositions and thus often decide by evaluating the most obvious aspect of an offer: price. This completes a vicious cycle: discouraged marketers come to believe that price is the only thing that matters to customers and thus close their minds to any possibility that they can learn anything new in their market.

However, we've seen companies armed with the right mind-set and tools gain new understandings of what customers want over and over again. These companies, many of which are featured in this book, have succeeded in extremely mature industries with extremely cynical customers.

We call these new understandings *insights,* and they are the fountain from which all great marketing flows. This chapter will profile several of these stories of insight.

You'll learn how marketers with extreme curiosity and simple-to-understand techniques have transformed industries as old as hotels, books, and mouthwash. We'll show you how a simple question can help you uncover customer needs that you and your competitors have missed for decades—or longer. And we'll show you some creative ways to get your customers to humor your newfound inquisitiveness long enough for you to develop new value propositions—offers they will find refreshingly different from those of your competitors.

DOES THE COMMONLY ACCEPTED BENEFITS (CAB)-BAGE TRAP EXIST IN YOUR INDUSTRY?

Our client was perplexed. The brand team had spent a lot of money researching a great way to position the company's new product but couldn't find a unique angle.

The product, a late entrant into a mental health drug market, was considered by potential prescribers to have *no* distinguishing differences from the competitor's medicines. So the client called us in to help the team figure out how to meet this challenge of standing out in a very crowded market.

The first thing we did was assess the method of research the company used and determine what it was designed to uncover. We were not surprised by what we found. The company had *assumed* what doctors' needs were and asked them to evaluate the new product on these perceived needs: *efficacy* of the medicine, its *safety* profile, and evidence of patient's *tolerability* of any side effects in clinical trials.

Whether they are selling prescription or generic drugs, medical devices or supplies, many health care marketers seem to believe that the only thing that matters to clinicians are these three factors: efficacy, safety, and tolerability. And these *are* important needs to address. *Every* medicine needs to work, be safe to use, and have manageable side effects.

But unless you are lucky enough to be marketing a rare blockbuster drug—one that makes a significant leap forward in any of these three areas—you have to be more strategically creative.

The truth is, most new medicines are only marginally better at delivering on one of these big three. Efficacy, safety, and tolerability are simply the table stakes to enter the market. They're usually not a source of differentiation.

If they don't get a broader sense of what prescribers really need, health care marketers fixate on investing in gaining high share of voice (SOV). SOV measures who is spending the most to loudly proclaim an efficacy, safety, and/or tolerability advantage.

Eventually, prescribers tune out pharmaceutical companies' constant claims of their drugs being more efficacious, being safer, and having fewer side effects. This results in prescriber cynicism and leads health care marketers to the false conclusion that the only way to get doctors to try a new drug is through lavish dinners, all-expenses-paid conferences, and various other boondoggles (which, in many cases, is no longer allowed).

We call this whole scenario the commonly accepted benefits (CAB-bage) trap. Like old cabbage, these wilted, worn-out types of benefits sought are bland and not capable of inspiring any kind of creative, fresh approaches. CAB-bage-like benefits sought exist in most industries and lead marketers to the false conclusion that only price or price-related benefits matter to customers.

There is a way out of the CAB-bage trap. It requires that you gain unique insight into stakeholders' needs *early* in the process of building a marketing plan.

Your ability to successfully use the rest of the tools in this book and your success in creating a differentiating marketing plan—indeed, the heights you will achieve as a marketer—depend on uncovering insights. This is why we titled this chapter "The Fountain from Which All Great Marketing Flows."

SPOKEN NEEDS, LATENT WANTS, PSYCHOSOCIAL VALUES, AND OTHER CONFUSING CONCEPTS SIMPLIFIED

Gaining insight is not easy, but we'll show you what you need to know to uncover it. But first, let's clarify and simplify the often confusing and overlapping definitions that surround this topic.

We will start with the end goal of the process in mind. What is a definition of *insight* according to Merriam-Webster's dictionary?

> in·sight
> *noun* \ˈin-ˌsīt\
> : the ability to understand people and situations in a very clear way
> : an understanding of the true nature of something

In our experience, *business* insights are typically *new* discoveries that competitors haven't addressed. If properly satisfied, insights can lead to a profitable competitive advantage for a company.

For example, the fact that prescribers desire efficacy, safety, and tolerability is not a new discovery about doctors; therefore, it is not an insight. But what if our pharmaceutical client profiled earlier had discovered the following?

Many clinicians consider improvement of mental patient's social skills to be a critical component in becoming a productive member of society.

If this is a new discovery about a key stakeholder *and* your industry is not properly addressing the idea itself—*and* if you think you might have the capabilities to do so—then it is an *insight*.

Could your product and its surrounding services deliver some benefits and services that uniquely help patients with their social skills? If yes, now you have an idea to explore instead of just screaming louder about efficacy, safety, and tolerability.

The insights-gaining process beseeches marketers to discover something *new* about customers. But how do you generate insights? It starts with learning what your customers are trying to achieve. Unfortunately, it's easy to get bogged down by a number of conflicting and overlapping definitions, such as *needs, wants, latent needs, psychosocial values,* and more, as you prepare to find this out.

So let's cut through the maze of terminology and define the three other terms that will deliver 98 percent of the value in ascertaining insights. Presented in a ladder format, each of the rungs in the ladder defines a concept that is more helpful in generating insights than the concept below it (Figure 2.1).

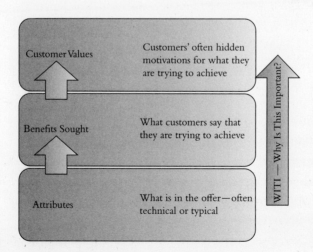

Figure 2.1 The Benefits Ladder

ATTRIBUTES CAN BE HELPFUL, SORT OF...

Attributes are the often technical-sounding ingredients in your product (e.g., reinforced polymers, antilock brakes) or the typical-sounding platitudes used to describe aspects of your product or service (e.g., 24/7 customer service, Six Sigma, our well-recognized brand name).

Many companies place too much emphasis on attributes in their marketing and sales communications. Just do a random review of company websites, and you'll find this to be true.

The problem with attributes when trying to generate insights is that they focus you too much on your products and not enough on what your customers *really want*. If you find yourself talking a great deal about the offer during the insight process, then you're in trouble—and miles away from the prize.

However, there's one way working with attributes *can* be helpful in the insight generation process: they can lead to uncovering benefits sought and customer values. For example, you could try the following:

- Write down a list of yours and your competitor's attributes.
- Then, for each attribute, ask the magical WITI question—"Why is this important?"

WITI is signified by the arrow beside the benefits ladder shown in Figure 2.1. The WITI concept was originally developed by Ralph Kennedy from Duke University in the decision analysis literature, and subsequently adopted to the analysis of customer value by Michel Tuan Pham, Kravis Professor of Business at Columbia University. WITI is magical because asking it can turn an attribute into a benefits sought, and, as we will see in a minute, can turn a benefits sought into a value.

Try it. Why is the attribute of antilock brakes important? Because it helps drivers *be safe in all types of driving conditions,* something many automobile purchasers would say they are trying to achieve, thereby fitting the definition of a benefit sought.

So working with attributes *can* lead you to discover customer benefits sought and values. However, it is less insightful than the methods we describe next. So if these more direct approaches are paying off, it's okay to skip attributes altogether when using a Benefits Ladder.

BENEFITS SOUGHT AND THE "HELP ME TO..." INSIGHT TECHNIQUE

Benefits sought are often very valuable in generating insights. They are the tangible, rational, and measurable things that customers claim they are trying to achieve in their business, personal life, and/or product category that's captured their interest.

They're often easy for customers to talk about, so the definition of the term includes what are typically called *spoken wants and needs.* Using a technique we call "help me to" can prompt customers to speak in benefits sought terms immediately without having to discuss attributes at all.

The "help me to" approach is simple. You merely ask a customer the following: "What do your favorite suppliers, vendors, and partners *help you to* do in your business?"

The answers you get to this question will likely be tangible, rational, and measurable benefits sought. You gain insight by gathering all the important CAB-bage benefits sought, *while also looking for new discoveries.* For example, doctors will tell you they like to work with pharmaceutical companies that help them heal patients by providing efficacious, safe, and tolerable drugs. None of that comes as a surprise. CAB-bage alert!

These are likely things that *any* player in a mature market must address. Write down these CAB-bage benefits sought, but keep going. By probing the customer for "What else?" and asking them to think more broadly, you can find some pearls. For example, you can ask doctors to think about the things that advisors, office supply vendors, employees, and so on, do that they really value. You can also ask them to speak about the specific and broader aspects of what they enjoy helping patients to do.

To illustrate this point, consider our chapter-opening case study. If asking some initial "help me to" questions to psychiatrists revealed the same-old CAB-bage benefits, one could broaden the discussion to include situations *outside* the realm of pharmaceuticals.

Imagine that after some consideration, one psychiatrist blurts out, "Well, I really value being able to counsel my patients on how to deal with common social situations that they have trouble with . . ." *Bingo!* You may be on the track of the insight highlighted earlier, especially if your product or service can uniquely address the finding:

Insight: Many clinicians consider improvement of mental patient's social skills to be a critical component in becoming a productive member of society.

CUSTOMER VALUES ARE OFTEN UNSPOKEN AND CAN EXPLAIN STRANGE CUSTOMER BEHAVIORS

Values are often intangible, emotional, and difficult to measure. They are typically considered unspoken needs, because they lie below the surface of a customer's consciousness. Therefore, they require a bit of effort to unearth.

But if you can uncover them *and* uniquely address them, values lead to the most powerful insights, because they explain customers' true motivations.

In fact, values are so powerful that companies who address them can get customers to behave in seemingly irrational ways. For example, in the 1970s and 1980s, IBM was able to successfully sell what some believed to be inferior computer hardware systems to business customers. It was successful in doing so because buyers wanted to feel the safety of dealing with a known brand name in a rapidly changing field. Ask anyone who worked in the information technology business during this era, and he or she will remember the power of the saying, "No one ever got fired for buying IBM."

A similar issue exists today with Apple products, particularly the iPhone. Many technologists are at a loss to explain the rabid allegiance of iPhone customers when they believe that technologically superior products from Samsung and others exist.

But Apple products have historically appealed to the "think different" crowd, segments of customers who want to feel that they a part of a counterculture. This is a value that Apple has uniquely addressed in the past—and one that's hard to combat on the basis of features and functions alone.

So how does one uncover customers' values? Once again, by using the WITI question. If customers state that they are seeking a rational, tangible, measurable benefits sought, you keep asking, "Why is that important?" until they say something emotional, intangible, and hard to measure.

INQUIRE BROADLY WHEN SEARCHING FOR VALUES IN A BUSINESS-TO-BUSINESS-TO-CONSUMER SITUATION

The same rules discussed above regarding benefits sought—inquiring broadly to uncover insights—are very important in uncovering values in business-to-business (B2B) and business-to-business-to-consumer (B2B2C) markets. Rene Gilvert, a vice president of global marketing at Takeda Pharmaceuticals, has led some highly successful, insight-driven brand strategies targeting large health insurance administrators (payers) and specialist physicians. We asked him for the secrets to his success.

"In a complex environment, it's often hard to uncover insights, even in industries one knows very well. This may even extend to research companies, who tend to ask the same questions of our clients, yielding the same old research findings about needs," Rene told us.

"The key is to push beyond your core product to thinking about your clients' entire life at work—and maybe even their life beyond work. It's this kind of thinking that generates new ideas that competitors miss. It's easy to say 'Why bother?' when thinking about areas that your current value proposition doesn't address. But this is where we've found several big opportunities."

We couldn't have said it better ourselves. On that note, let's continue our previous mental health drug example. When you ask why it's important to the psychiatrist to help patients with their social skills, he or she might say, "I like to feel like my practice's overall interaction with patients is helping them integrate into society better."

The value? "Helping patients integrate into society." It's emotion-based and difficult to measure, but it's a powerful motivator. If this physician felt that one particular company's value proposition did a better job of helping patients achieve this, he or she would certainly be more likely to recommend that company's products, even at a higher price than that of a competitor's.

CLIMBING THE LADDER WITH SKIN CREAM

Let's look at how a Benefits Ladder might work with a straightforward product like skin cream (Figure 2.2).

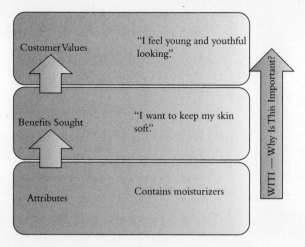

Figure 2.2 Skin Cream Benefits Ladder

This example helps us make some crucial points. First, marketing a skin cream based on the attribute that it contains moisturizers hardly sets it apart from any other product on the market. So attribute-driven marketing is simply not effective and doesn't tell us much about what the customer is trying to achieve.

However, imagine that we ask a woman what her favorite beauty products help her to do (the "help me to" technique). It's not hard to imagine one response being, "They help keep my skin soft." Soft skin is an example of a tangible, rational, measurable benefit sought; after all, you can certainly touch and feel soft skin!

Is this an insight, though? Probably not. At this mature stage of the skin cream market, delivering on soft skin is most likely a CAB-bage benefit sought, unless a company develops a new blockbuster product that delivers a huge leap ahead in this area.

In the absence of an insight, one would attempt to further climb the benefits ladder by asking the question, "*Why* is soft skin important?" You can imagine that after stating a few other benefits sought (e.g., "I don't want my clothes to chafe against my skin"), we would get to the statement, "I want to feel like I did when I was younger." This not-so-easily-uncovered emotional, difficult-to-measure feeling is a *value*.

The best marketers understand the power of appealing to values. As of this writing, the top skin cream in the very lucrative and competitive U.S. market is

Olay™ Creams - For Healthy & Younger Looking Skin
www.olay.com/NewRegeneristFormula
America's #1 Selling Anti Aging Moisturiser Got Better. More Here

Figure 2.3   Olay Banner Ad

Olay. A quick Google search for skin cream reveals the Olay banner ad shown in Figure 2.3.

Let's look at some great insight-based marketing case studies in a few other mature businesses, often the toughest industries for marketers to get out of the CAB-bage trap.

ONE GOOD INSIGHT STRATEGY AFTER ANOTHER: THE HISTORY OF LISTERINE

Amazingly, in a decade where self-driving cars, genetic mapping, and customized radio stations are a reality, the number 1 selling mouthwash is a brand introduced in 1881. Listerine is a testament to what is possible when a good product—but not the clear-cut *best* product—relentlessly looks for new benefits sought and motivating values to claim in its strategies.

After being sold only to dentists as an antiseptic for its first 20 years, the Listerine brand became one of the world's first prescription products released for sale in pharmacies direct to consumers (over the counter).

The discovery that Listerine freshened one's breath potentially moved the product's appeal beyond germophobes. Most marketers simply would have positioned the product as the cure for bad breath and waited for the sales to roll in. But the very astute brand marketers at Listerine did some research and discovered an insight: *there was a cultural stigma around the affliction of bad breath, and no one wanted to talk about it, admit they had it, or deal with the consequences.*

To counter the avoidance factor for a taboo subject, Listerine *created* a medical condition in 1921 to give bad breath sufferers validity. Listerine brand marketers coined the condition *halitosis,* a term that's now a part of the English dictionary.

Listerine's creation of a new disease category has been successfully duplicated in other markets recently. One example is Paxil's approach for legitimizing depression in Japan (*Kokoro no Kaze,* meaning "depression is a cold of the soul"). Another is a campaign by a company that sells a drug to aid smokers in giving up cigarettes. It is seeking to position nicotine addiction as a disease or medical condition that can be beyond the reach of self-discipline. The goal is to convince insurance and other health industry payers to reimburse patients for the cost of the drug.

But even after legitimizing the affliction of bad breath, the Listerine team apparently wasn't satisfied. Curing halitosis to simply deliver the functional benefit sought of "freshen up my bad breath" wasn't strong enough. They wanted to ladder up to an emotional value to further strengthen Listerine's appeal. They tied their messages to the intangible *values* of *love, romance,* and *strong relationships.*

Specifically, the 1920s and 1930s era ads had strong, although somewhat negative, emotional appeals that included headlines such as "Breath Only a Mother Could Love." In one poignant campaign aimed at young women, Listerine actually introduced the world to the phrase "always a bridesmaid, never a bride" in alluding to halitosis as a possible reason why an otherwise attractive woman was still single!

These insight-based strategies helped catapult the brand to a dominant position. Even more important, they seemed to instill a habit of never resting on the brand's laurels. This attitude has kept Listerine in the number 1 position despite fierce competition.

Perhaps the toughest competition for the brand came with the 1960s introduction of the nonmedicinal, better-tasting Scope. Listerine's initial reaction to the new competitor was to up the ante on claims it had made since about 1941: that gargling with Listerine could also help fight colds and sore throats. The Federal Trade Commission put a stop to these claims with a ruling in 1974 that stated there was no evidence to support them.

Undaunted, Listerine's unrelenting quest for consumer insight led its marketing team to successfully combat Scope's legitimate claims that its product tasted better. They discovered that strong medicinal qualities in certain product categories were an indication to many customers that the product was working.

With the establishment of halitosis as a legitimate condition that consumers felt shouldn't be "left to chance," Listerine's new marketing focused on the value of *security.* Leapfrogging Scope's claim of tasting better, Listerine's positioning communicated, in essence, "if a mouthwash has a strong taste, this is how you know it's working."

The resulting 1969 campaign, called Hate/Love, communicated the message, "I hate it, but I love it twice a day." As always, appealing to values trumped

Scope's better tasting benefits sought–oriented claim, and Listerine's market share grew even more.

Listerine's success continues to the present day. New insights continue to drive functional messages when the brand has new claims or inventions, from fighting gingivitis to new product forms such as oral strips and plaque-detecting rinses for children.

Still, Listerine's most powerful appeals are emotional and values-based—such as linking the use of the product to a positive daily discipline in the "hang in there for the full 60 seconds of swishing" commercials.

Listed here are some of the insights that have driven the success of the Listerine brand in a very competitive market for more than 125 years:

Insight: People are embarrassed by bad breath and need a medical explanation for the condition to feel comfortable enough to address it.

Insight: People may not realize that the reason they are missing important opportunities in their lives is due to bad breath.

Insight: Busy people appreciate products that help them deal with multiple issues (e.g., freshens breath, fights colds and sore throats [from the 1940s to 1960s], freshens breath and fights gingivitis [from the 1980s]).

Insight: Consumers want their personal care products in highly emotional categories to deliver strong evidence that they are working, even if the experience is unpleasant.

Insight: Consumers appreciate portable products that allow them to effectively freshen up when they are on the go (e.g., Listerine breath strips).

Insight: As exercise has become more and more popular, consumers can relate to the notion of no pain, no gain (the "hang in there" campaign mentioned previously).

After studying this case, do you still think that your customers care only about your industry's commonly accepted CAB-bage benefits sought?

FINDING THE INSIGHT IN A LEISURELY TRIP TO THE BOOKSTORE

As this is being written in 2013, consumer electronics retailers are the latest industry worried about being Amazon-ed. Chains such as Best Buy are tired of being Amazon's showroom, a place where people can touch and feel products before ordering at a lower price from the online retailer.

Of course, bookstores were the original victim of Amazon's business model. Many independent stores and a few significant chains, such as Borders, have gone bankrupt as Amazon has grown.

However, one bookstore chain has weathered the storm better than all others, due to an insight it gained in the early 1990s. Ironically, the antidote to Amazon was discovered accidentally, *before* the site's founding in 1994.

The story begins with a man named Leonard Riggio, a bookstore owner, trying to find out why people were doing something strange in his bookstores: they were spending significantly more time when shopping for books than when shopping in other types of retail stores.

It would have been easy to leap to several assumptions from these data that would have led to different types of operational strategies:

SHOPPERS SPEND MORE TIME IN BOOKSTORES BECAUSE . . .

Assumption: They can't find what they are looking for.

Possible Strategy: Reduce the number of titles or increase help staff to help shoppers more quickly find what they need.

Assumption: Lines are too long, and shoppers can't check out their purchases efficiently.

Possible Strategy: Add checkout lines and increase cash register operators to get shoppers in and out of the store more quickly.

Assumption: Bookstores don't have the right titles, and it takes shoppers a long time to find a suitable substitute for what they originally came for.

Possible Strategy: Increase the number of titles to help people quickly find exactly what they are looking for.

Of course, all these seem like reasonable approaches to solve what appears to be an operational efficiency problem. But all these strategies to speed up the book shopper's experience would have been exactly the *wrong* move!

Fortunately, Riggio had the wisdom to ask customers *why* they were spending significant amounts of time in his stores. And as it turned out, it wasn't a problem at all.

What he found led to significant innovation in his bookshops:

Insight: "To book lovers, shopping for books is a form of entertainment, similar to going to the movies."

Based on this, Riggio's company, Barnes and Noble, did the *opposite* of operationally sterilizing its stores. Barnes and Noble looked to encourage shoppers' entertainment mentality by adding comfortable couches, chairs, and coffee shops that delivered a message of "stay awhile."

The result is that, unlike many of its now-bankrupt former competitors, Barnes and Noble has been able to thrive in the age of Amazon. Through an insight-based strategy that led to a value proposition that its biggest competitor can't deliver on—an entertainment experience—Barnes and Noble remains one of the few viable global competitors in the bricks-and-mortar bookstore market.

HOLIDAY INN EXPRESS "LADDERS UP" AND FINDS THE UNSPOKEN MOTIVATION FOR BEING A CHEAPSKATE

There seems to be no end to hotel innovation on the high end of the market. From the over-the-top opulence of Dubai's Burj Al Arab to Starwood's trendy W chain, hoteliers can serve up lots of different value propositions for people willing to spend several hundred dollars a night or more.

A much more difficult nut to crack is in the value-oriented hotel segments. New Web-based travel agents, such as Priceline and Expedia, can quickly serve up scores of attractively priced hotel options for any given night and locality.

So, when a value-priced chain differentiates itself successfully in this unforgiving, price-centric category, it's worthy of study. And that is exactly what Holiday Inn Express (HIE), launched in 1990, has done.

Positioned to serve as a smaller version of the flagship Holiday Inn properties but with fewer amenities, the Express brand courted price-conscious business travelers as a primary target. In an effort to provide something unique for this segment, HIE marketers conducted research to figure out what target customers wanted *besides* a competitive rate that would save money for their companies.

There can be few more frustrating tasks than trying to discover additional benefits sought from customers who are, by their very definition, price-conscious. Indeed, their price-sensitivity can actually become even more acute when it comes to business travel. They do not want to be called on the carpet by the cost-conscious finance personnel that review their expense reports when they return home.

The HIE marketers persisted in finding out *what else* was driving the hotel decisions made by the price-conscious business traveler. Surely there were some other criteria besides price that mattered!

And they were right; the team's persistence paid off. Because these travelers arrived late and left early to the hotels they stayed in, they appreciated hotels that helped them by providing a *minimum level of amenities* that truly mattered.

Based on this information, the HIE team decided to refrain from installing pools, elaborate exercise facilities, and spa services in their hotels in exchange for the simple mix of free Internet, a great shower experience, and a free breakfast. This just right value proposition immediately appealed to the segment's extreme pragmatism.

As we saw in the Listerine story, HIE marketers also weren't happy with a functional-only, benefits sought value proposition. They wanted to discover the emotional, motivating value driving ultra cost-sensitivity.

By relentlessly asking the WITI question to target customers, HIE marketers uncovered a key psychological component of cheapskate-ism:

Insight: Price-conscious people believe that they are too smart to be taken advantage of.

How does this simple insight translate into a winning marketing strategy? By presenting Holiday Inn Express as the smart choice of price-conscious business travelers, with a just right value proposition, the chain has avoided being just another hotel chain positioning itself as a low-priced hotel for price-conscious business travelers.

Its "Stay Smart" tagline and advertising campaign continues to be highly memorable and effective. Featuring a variety of humorous 30- to 60-second spots, ordinary people accomplish extraordinary things that cause them to be misidentified as experts. A layperson mistaken for a doctor saves a brain surgery patient; a parent visiting his daughter at college solves an "unsolvable" math problem and is mistaken for a professor; a man in a towel beats a chess champion and designs an invisible fighter jet all before his shower in the morning.

The HIE catchphrase, always delivered at the end of the commercial, has become part of American pop culture: "No, I'm not a (brain surgeon, mathematics professor, chess champion), but I did stay at a Holiday Inn Express last night!"

The combination of the Stay Smart message and the just right value proposition appeals to the pragmatic and emotional sides of the target segment. As a result, the company grew at twice the rate of any other brand in the limited service segment and continues to thrive today. HIE brand awareness in the United States stands at nearly 100 percent.

Perhaps the most important outcome for the HIE strategy is that HIE was able to make an emotional connection with a segment that, many would say, is not vulnerable to emotional appeals. HIE makes its customers feel smart, which enables the chain to thrive—amazingly, *without* being the lowest-priced provider in the segment!

A TOOL, FOUR WORDS, AND PERSISTENCE: THE BENEFITS LADDER AND AN INQUISITIVE MIND ARE ALL YOU NEED TO UNLOCK INSIGHT

The Benefits Ladder, shown in Figure 2.4, is a tool you can use to uncover your key stakeholders' values and benefits sought.

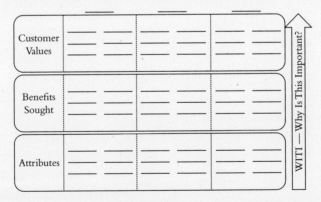

Figure 2.4   Benefits Ladder Template

Source: Copyright © 2014 Impact Planning Group. All rights reserved.

(*continued*)

(*continued*)

The template provides a space for collecting values, benefits sought, and if necessary, attributes for up to three important stakeholders that you identified on your influence map from Chapter 1.

Although salespeople or other knowledgeable personnel might be able to approximate the benefits ladder information on behalf of customers, there is *no substitute* for direct customer interaction. In fact, this is so critical that we are going to assume you will seek out customer interviews to construct your benefits ladder. The following will guide you in how to direct your customer conversations.

QUESTIONING TECHNIQUES

Step 1: First, tell the customer that you are having this discussion because you believe that, by understanding his or her company better, your company will be able to provide more valuable and innovative services. Then, ask the following question:

"Think about your best partners, suppliers, and vendors. What do they help you to do in your business that you value the most?"

This will most likely start a conversation that elicits a set of tangible, rational, measurable benefits sought. *Write them all down.* You may not even need to fill any attributes into your benefits ladder at all.

Step 2: As you collect the benefits sought, ask the four-word question "Why is that important?" often. For example, if a customer says, "We value a relationship with a partner who provides us with best practices information in our industry," you might ask, "Why is gathering best practices information important?"

Eventually, you will hear some intangible, emotional, hard-to-measure value statements, such as, "This kind of best practices information makes us feel confident that we are optimizing our operation and keeping at the forefront of our industry, which secures the future of this 50-year-old, family-owned business." You can see how the values of confidence, industry leadership, security, and stewardship are all contained in that one sentence.

Write down all the benefits sought and values that you uncover in the appropriate section of your benefits ladder. Volume is important at this point, so collect as many as your customer mentions during the interview.

PERSISTENCE

Armed with the aforementioned tool and the right questions, you are on the path to gaining insight. You have to be persistent now, and use some finesse in order to ask the same WITI questions repeatedly without upsetting your customer. But you can do it.

Step 3: Go for insights. You will require another level of stick-to-it-iveness to truly gain insight. Most of the benefits sought you will gather will be of the CAB-bage variety that we spoke of earlier in the chapter.

Therefore, discovering something *new* might require that you broaden the frame of your questioning. For example, you could say, "Think beyond the particular industry that my company represents, think beyond even your business; tell me about a time when you received great value in *any* areas of your life. What was that company or person helping you to do?"

Of course, this will likely lead to a more general discussion, which might make you feel like you aren't collecting benefits sought and values that matter to your business or industry. But collect them anyway. You are looking for insight, and it's this beyond CAB-bage type of benefit that will often unlock the path to differentiation.

You can see this persistence in action when harkening back to our chapter-opening example of the mental health drug. Remember this insight?

Insight: Many clinicians consider improvement of mental patient's social skills to be a critical component in becoming a productive member of society.

(continued)

(*continued*)

This psychiatrist was acknowledging the value he placed on his ability to counsel patients on social skills. He made this comment at the end of a long interview that mostly centered on efficacy, safety, and tolerability benefits sought, after the interviewer broadened the questioning scope.

The pharmaceutical company ultimately leveraged this insight to differentiate its value proposition. It developed services around its medicine offer that helped elicit mental health patients' improved social skills.

TURN BENEFITS SOUGHT AND VALUES INTO *INSIGHT*

Your job as a marketer is to analyze all the information you have and figure out what the true insight is. This requires that you find the most powerful, non-CAB-bage benefits sought or emotional value and use it to create an insight statement.

This statement should not talk about your product or service but rather highlight the following (from our earlier definition of insight): *a new discovery about a customer or stakeholder that, if properly addressed, can lead to a profitable competitive advantage for your company.*

You'll know you have it right if the insight immediately leads to some creative ideas for differentiating your product or service. Review all the insights statements in this chapter to get a well-rounded feel for the process.

RESEARCH

None of this insight-discovering business is easy. Research companies can be helpful partners, but pay attention to an important best practice if you use them: create a *customers' benefits sought hypothesis* first that includes some non-CAB-bage benefits, before the research. Otherwise, the research company may come back to you with output that lacks insight. Remember the example of our client at the beginning of this chapter? The company spent loads of research money, only to find it wasn't differentiated from its competitors on CAB-bage benefits!

Working with your hypothesized benefits sought, the research company can determine if they are truly important to your customers, while also seeking to uncover other benefits sought that you *haven't* thought of.

EVEN AGRICULTURAL PRODUCT DISTRIBUTORS IN RURAL VIETNAM WILL PARTICIPATE IN A CARD SORT

Developing a pre-research hypothesis is a good idea even if you are doing the research yourself, without a research company's help. We found this out when assisting an agricultural products company in improving its business performance in Vietnam.

In our initial meeting in Ho Chi Minh City, we asked some of the company's sales personnel to share with us their knowledge of distributors' needs. This helped us hypothesize and then prioritize a list of five or six benefits sought that seemed to be the most important. We then wrote each one on its own index card, added two blank index cards to the pack, and headed out to visit some distributors.

We explained at the start of each distributor interview that our aim was to understand and serve them better. We posed some high-level questions, then handed them the stack of index cards and asked them to sort the cards in order of importance. We then had them add two or more benefits sought on the blank cards and prioritize them.

Not surprisingly to us (but to the astonishment of our client), every distributor enthusiastically participated in the exercise. We quickly obtained a prioritized list of benefits sought and some new insights that changed the way the company was working with distributors.

Here is the more important point: if we can get distributors in rural Vietnam to participate in a card sort, you can *certainly* get your customers to talk more to you. If you learn nothing else from this chapter, at least hear this: to achieve marketing excellence, you must *speak with your customers more frequently.* We hope the lessons in this chapter have given you a new appreciation for what it means to uncover what customers want. We hope you also now understand why we believe that insight is the fountain from which all great marketing flows.

But not all customers want the same things. That's a reality that we will address—and embrace—in the next chapter. The exciting concept of segmentation that will be discussed in Chapter 3 builds on the foundation that the Benefits Ladder establishes. Read on!

CHAPTER 3

Are You Making Lukewarm Tea?

How a Medical Diagnostics Marketer Blew Up Its "Average" Product and Got a Positive Result

POWER TOOL: NEEDS-BASED SEGMENTATION

Whenever you find yourself on the side of the majority, it is time to pause and reflect.
—Mark Twain, American author and humorist

CAPITALIZING ON DIFFERENCES IN CUSTOMER NEEDS IS A BIG OPPORTUNITY

Needs-based segmentation is the process of dividing your customers into *nonobvious, unique, customer-defined, insight-driving* groups for purposes of creating specific offerings for each group. Many companies think that they already comprehend segmentation and execute it well. But the fact is that a mere 5 percent—perhaps even fewer—of the companies we work with really understand how this approach differs from the way they're already segmenting.

We see these organizations make the same, fundamental mistakes over and over again. Most often, they consider only demographic or other overly

37

simplistic approaches that merely *classify* customers. This results in a superficial understanding of true needs and drivers.

Conversely, we see remarkable results when companies truly segment based on customer needs. As such, we believe that needs-based segmentation is marketing's least understood and most underrated idea.

This chapter tells the story of a company that utilized the concept of needs-based segmentation with rare amounts of simplicity, power, and effectiveness. Although San Diego–based diagnostics marketer Quidel may not carry the same star power as Dell, Apple, and other chapter case studies, its story succinctly illustrates the secrets that most segmentation practitioners easily miss.

There is a vast upside of learning to do the type of segmentation we'll outline in the pages to come. The Quidel example shows how it leads to an endless string of ideas for developing differentiated products and services your customers love, which makes the job of building great value propositions much easier for even inexperienced marketers. It improves sales performance by making explicit the intuitive approach all great salespeople take, thereby allowing lesser performers to model it.

We will show you where you can find data proving that companies successfully practicing needs-based segmentation enjoy better financial performance. We'll also discuss how to marshal the internal company forces that can otherwise doom the execution of even properly conceived segmentation approaches.

Given the mistakes in approach we constantly see, doing needs-based segmentation correctly will leave you with a hugely advantageous strategy in your industry.

SEGMENTATION IS *NOT* MERELY A CONSUMER MARKETING CONCEPT

Perhaps the biggest misperception of all about needs-based segmentation is that it applies only to consumer marketing situations. We'll show you at the end of the Quidel story—and in this chapter's tools section—why we think segmentation is *even more powerful* for business-to-business (B2B) marketers. But don't skip the Quidel story; it has been a catalyst of segmentation ideas for many of the B2B marketers with whom we've shared the case in workshops over the years.

A PREGNANCY TEST YIELDS UNWELCOME NEWS FOR A GROUP OF B2B MARKETING EXPERTS

When Quidel Corporation acquired a new company in the early 1990s, it inherited a product line that was different than what it was used to. Quidel previously had a high success rate for in-doctor's-office ovulation tests, where they had almost an 80 percent share of the $6 million U.S. market.

The recent acquisition came with a home-based pregnancy test kit product that could be sold directly to consumers via retail outlets. However, Quidel was a very small player in the $20 million U.S. consumer pregnancy test market.

"Our competency was in calling on doctors and hospitals to promote our tests," explained Bob Gergen, a Quidel marketer at the time and now vice president of sales for Rapid Pathogen Screening. "But when Steven Frankel joined our organization as CEO [chief executive officer], he convinced us to take a chance on expanding in the consumer market." Frankel had experience in consumer markets prior to his joining Quidel.

So the company began to explore any ideas that would help differentiate its product and improve retail performance.

Exploring options in this case was quite an unusual step. The combination of an acquired product, a different market than a company is used to, and a comparatively low share is usually all the reason a company needs to ignore the product on its way to a certain death.

A QUICK ASIDE

PRODUCTS WITH NO CLEAR COMPETITIVE ADVANTAGE ARE SOMETIMES THE BEST OPPORTUNITIES TO EXPERIMENT WITH NEEDS-BASED SEGMENTATION

In our experience, the types of situations like the one Quidel encountered are perfect fixer-up opportunities for testing new segmentation approaches. This is because they can provide a low-risk test to determine how a needs-based approach can offer opportunities in difficult markets.

(continued)

(continued)

For example, we worked with a pharmaceutical product that treated a rare cellular disease. That was the good news. The bad news was much more prevalent: the product was late to market, faced an entrenched well-known competitor with a reputation as experienced experts on the disease, and apparently had no unique features and benefits, other than providing a second option to doctors and patients.

After an exhaustive, mostly fruitless search for some strategic approaches that could differentiate the product, we discovered that our client's product had a plant-based biology, whereas the competitor's product was based in the pituitary glands of rats!

This wasn't quite enough for doctors or patients to consider switching from a drug that had been their only option. However, the marketing team looked for a nonobvious, unique, customer-defined, insight-driving group that might care about the product's base biology.

Their research led them to a small, niche patient segment they called Naturalists. These were sufferers of the aforementioned cell disease who were extremely careful about all aspects of their diet and nutrition. The team built a case for the new drug by first convincing doctors that its product had the same efficacy, safety, and tolerability profile as the existing drug. Next, they taught the doctors how to identify prototypical Naturalist patients and ultimately how to present the plant-based biology as a reason to switch to the new drug.

This approach provided some breathing room for a product that seemed to have no chance at all for success.

NEEDS-BASED SEGMENTATION IS ABOUT MUCH MORE THAN JUST FINDING NICHES

Unlike the cellular disease drug marketers discussed in the sidebar, Quidel was looking for more than a niche. The product was already performing like a niche product.

What Quidel wanted was to grow the product's share bigger, so they set out to find some new ideas to make it happen. They discovered a way to segment that allowed them to create different value propositions for different groups: a hugely successful, multisegment (rather than a single-segment niche) approach. Almost immediately, new customers who hadn't even noticed Quidel's product in the past now purchased it. How Quidel's team built such a successful strategy was a journey that included several epiphanies.

The Lukewarm Tea Syndrome

In looking for answers to grow the share of its home pregnancy test product, Quidel marketers realized that there was a problem with the way it and its competitors were thinking about the home pregnancy test market. All were assuming that a single offering had to appeal to every customer. Therefore, each company, including Quidel, was offering a single brand that attempted to capture as large a share of the market as possible.

We call this the *lukewarm tea syndrome,* which describes most companies' tendency to make watered-down value propositions that appeal to no one. The analogy suggests that, in the market for tea, if some customers prefer hot tea and some prefer cold tea, the mythical company averages the result and makes lukewarm tea. No one is satisfied, and customers move on to an offering that better matches their needs.

The Quidel team realized that if they could define important differences between women of childbearing age, they might be able to unlock opportunity by defining these segments and creating tailored offers. Although they found it impractical (and unnecessary) to change the core tests for different segments, they could customize the packaging, promotion, and price for each group of women.

The trick would be in finding a delicate balance: not overwhelming the company's operations by creating too many segments and customized value propositions, but doing enough to cause customers in each segment to feel that they had a product designed especially for them.

The answers would come through the wisdom to not declare victory too soon—and a seventeenth-century theory applied to a modern business problem.

Segmentation Dimensions: Time to Pause and Reflect

The Quidel team set out to define the answers to a couple of key segmentation questions: *Why* did different customers want different things? What were their *underlying motivations?*

A best practice in the quest to segment is to use binary descriptors to explain the differences between good prospects for a product. *Binary* refers to descriptors that show stark variations among customers with very little gray area in between.

This makes it easier to profile and identify customers in each segment and design specific value propositions that appeal to each uniquely. Just finding one or two good binary descriptors can lead to very successful segmentation approaches.

We call these binary descriptors segmentation dimensions and recommend that you develop them by completing as many variations of the following statement as possible: "Some good customers are _____ (fill in a characteristic attitude, behavior, motivation, or need here), while other, different good customers are _____ (fill in a different or opposite characteristic attitude, behavior, motivation or need)."

But not just any characteristics will work here. Description-based segmentation dimensions (which we call classifications) don't provide much insight, which is why Quidel rejected several, if they considered them at all:

REJECTED SEGMENTATION (CLASSIFICATION) DIMENSIONS

"Some good customers are _____, while other, different good customers are _____."

- Rich women versus poor women
- Urban dwellers versus rural
- Young women versus older women
- Religious women versus less religious women

These classifications don't offer much insight into customer needs and are also easily copied by competitors.

Paraphrasing Mark Twain's famous quote from the opening of this chapter, "When you suspect you are segmenting like the majority of your competitors, it's time to pause and reflect." The Quidel team looked for something more insightful, and their determination paid big dividends.

The Eureka Moment: Finding Customer-Defined, Insightful, Actionable, Practical, Why-Based Segments

By refusing to settle for the obvious, Quidel's segmentation quest forced the team to dig deeper to uncover differences in motivations among women in this market. Companies not willing to settle for obvious, stale segmentation approaches attempt to answer *why- and what-based* questions regarding customer needs, such as:

- Why do different customers want different things?
- What different things are they trying to accomplish?
- What are the differences in attitudes, behaviors, and motivations among customers who want different things?

In the case of Quidel, this drove the consideration of some new segmentation dimensions:

GOOD POTENTIAL SEGMENTATION DIMENSIONS

"Some good customers are _____, while other, different good customers are _____."

- Organized women versus forgetful women
- Career-driven versus family-focused
- Outgoing personalities versus shy personalities
- "Get it done fast" versus "get it done right"
- "Want to be pregnant" versus "don't want to be pregnant"

Quidel could be pretty sure that dimensions such as these were unique, because no other company seemed to be recognizing these types of differences in their value propositions. But the next question after developing good, needs-based, nonclassification binary dimensions of segmentation is still, which dimension is best to use in segmenting customers? To answer this, you can turn to the work of one Sir William Hamilton.

Using Occam's Razor to Select the Best Approach to Segmentation

Occam's razor, first postulated in 1852 by Sir William Hamilton, essentially states that one should stick with the simplest possible theory until a theory with greater explanatory power is uncovered. This is a great rule to keep in mind in many areas of life and business, but especially when choosing between several possible segmentation dimensions. It simplifies the approach's communication and implementation.

Specifically, teams should look for the *simplest segmentation dimension* that explains a very different set of experiences and needs. According to Bob Gergen, that means the last in the list of good dimensions listed: women who want to be pregnant versus women who don't want to be pregnant.

"We especially liked the idea of a product for women who want to be pregnant, since it was what women were trying to achieve," Bob said. Also, Quidel realized it could target a product for the other side of the binary dimension.

Good approaches always feature easily derived profiles of each segment that show the stark differences between them in attitudes, behaviors, and needs. Consider the following:

Segment 1: The woman who wants to be pregnant is dreaming of a happy future. She's willing to talk to anyone about her plans. She whimsically strolls through the baby products aisle, often before having any children at all. When she buys the product, she *hopes for a positive* result.

Segment 2: The woman who doesn't want to be pregnant is tense. She probably keeps her thoughts of being pregnant private. She avoids the baby products aisle, not wishing to be reminded that she may be facing an unplanned, major event in her life. When she buys the product, she *fears a positive* result.

These stark differences in needs highlighted a big opportunity for the Quidel marketing team. Here was a simple, yet powerful segmentation that could easily be handled operationally with just *two* (instead of many) value propositions! The team had to be excited as they began to hypothesize how they could leverage these differences.

Getting Segmentation Right Makes Treating Different Customers Differently Much Easier

The goal of segmentation—developing value propositions that make different segments of customers feel like the product was designed uniquely for them—is made far easier when segments are needs based.

To prove the point, we'll challenge you to stop reading right now and design a different home pregnancy kit for each of the two segments, based solely on the segment descriptions provided. We bet that, regardless of your level of marketing experience, you could create different value propositions for each of these two segments across the 4 Ps (product, place, promotion, and price). Take a second before reading on, and ask yourself the following four questions:

- How would you name the home pregnancy kit differently for each of the two segments: the want to bes and the don't want to bes?
- If the pregnancy test kits are primarily bought in grocery and convenience stores, which department (place) inside the store would you merchandise the product for the want to bes versus the don't want to bes?
- How would you build excitement (promotion) for the products differently for each segment?
- Which segment would you charge more for the product (price)?

Here is how Quidel built on its segmentation insights to create two very different, very successful value propositions for each of the segments. Don't be surprised if your ideas were close to what is shown in Figure 3.1.

	Want to be pregnant segment		Don't want to be pregnant segment
Segment		V	
Product name	Conceive	V	RapidVue[1]
Package design	Blue/Pink, Baby pictures	V	Small, discreet, low key [2]
Located in	Baby products aisle [3]	V	Pharmaceutical section
Promotion	Free college education raffle	V	None[4]
Price	$9.99[5]	V	$6.99

1. If you fear an unwanted pregnancy, you want results fast.
2. Package was designed to be virtually unnoticed in the shopping basket.
3. Baby is yet to be born, but this is the section that the hopeful mother is browsing.
4. Promotions build excitement for a product, but this segment does not want to be excited.
5. After testing multiple test points, Quidel came to the conclusion that hope sells better than fear.

Figure 3.1   Quidel Pregnancy Test Value Proposition

Radically Different Offerings—without Changing the Core Product

We would like to remind you that Quidel created these clearly defined, clearly different value propositions *without changing the core product at all*. The basic test kit was virtually the same for both segments!

Marketers who have the ability to change the core product for different segments have yet another weapon to leverage in treating different customers differently.

A Positive Result with Both Segments: Quidel's Customers Vote with Their Pocketbooks

The question of what Quidel's customers thought of the approach is answered by its results. According to Bob Gergen, Quidel's segmented approach grew its home pregnancy test sales to $4 million in a total market of $20 million in three years. By our calculation, this is the equivalent of going from 0 percent to 25 percent market share in a very short period of time.

Quidel went from an averaged single, lukewarm product to two products that different segments felt was designed specifically for them. The want to bes felt good when they came upon the bright, baby-picture-laden test kit while they were browsing in the baby products section. The don't want to bes appreciated being able to buy a low-key package that promised fast results for a reasonable price.

Great Needs–Based Segmentation Immediately Raises the Effectiveness of Marketers—and Salespeople

But maybe the most incredible aspect of the story was that Quidel accomplished all of this with a marketing team outside its element. Amazingly, its experienced business-to-business (B2B) marketers found almost immediate success in a business-to-consumer (B2C) market.

Bob Gergen told us that, despite Quidel's newness in the channel, "retailers said that no other competitors were thinking this way. They loved our ideas and asked us 'What's next?'"

That's what great needs-based segmentation does for marketers and sales teams. It provides such a clear profile of differences between good customers that designing effective segment-based value propositions is easier. It immediately raises the effectiveness of the marketing team. It gives the sales team a fresh, creative, and interesting story to tell customers.

In B2B, professional sales-based situations, the best salespeople utilize needs-based segmentation intuitively. They instinctively sense the differences between good customers and tailor their messages to the buyers' situations. When marketing joins the party by developing different value proposition options for sales to present, it creates a salesperson's nirvana.

Perhaps even more important, needs-based segmentation approaches tend to make explicit what the greatest salespeople do intuitively. Now, sales reps with less talent or experience have a framework that helps them better understand customers. By learning to ask the right questions to segment a customer, and by being armed with a unique, segment-specific value proposition, mediocre reps quickly become good, and good reps become great.

Why This Concept Works *Better* in B2B Situations Than It Does in the Consumer Marketing World

Those who view needs-based segmentation as a consumer marketing concept are misguided. Unlike B2B marketers, consumer marketers typically don't have the opportunity to engage in dialogue with a prospect before they buy. It's a definite disadvantage that they don't get the opportunity to figure out what segment the customer is in before making a purchase and adjusting their pitch appropriately.

Consumer marketers taking a multisegment approach often have to rely on creating separate offerings that they *hope* the right customers find. Quidel's full value proposition maximized the chances of this happening.

What a huge advantage it is in a B2B situation to have a sales force to leverage throughout the entire segmentation process, from helping define meaningful customer differences to identifying which customers belong to which segment to ultimately presenting the customized value proposition to the right segment audience.

Columbia University Professor Larry Selden Has the Financial Proof of Segmentation's Power

In their 2003 book *Angel Customers & Demon Customers,* authors Larry Selden of Columbia University and Geoffrey Colvin studied the financial results of companies that had organized themselves around needs-based customer segments. Those that embraced the approach outperformed their peer groups on four important financial measurements that drive a company's price-to-earnings ratio (P/E).

According to Selden (perhaps the world's foremost expert on segmentation's financial benefits), there should be no remaining doubt that the concept makes sound business sense. However, its enemy is insidious and internal.

"We've already seen why it [organizing companies around groups of customers] makes sense from a *logical* point of view . . . [along with] powerful *financial* reasons for organizing the company around customer segments," Selden says in *Angel Customers & Demon Customers.* "One reason [companies] don't try [it] is it would mean changing who's accountable for what."[1]

Not Only Should You Involve the Sales Force In the Initiative but You Risk Expensive Failure if You Don't

Our own experience allows us to be even more specific about the type of internal conflict that torpedoes this powerful concept. The primary problem is that marketers go too far into the segmentation process without involving the sales force, who become frightened that they are losing accountability for a key customer initiative.

We have seen countless sales teams reject otherwise strong segmentation approaches because they feel that understanding customer differences is *their* job, not marketing's. However, the solution is straightforward.

We have never seen an approach fail when a few respected members of the sales team were involved in the project as partners from the beginning. As you work through the tools we are about to outline, make sure that you include respected salespeople in every step.

---

[1] From Larry Selden and Geoffrey Colvin's *Angel Customers & Demon Customers,* pages 92 and 114. Full citation of the book is available in the Chapter 3 Book Notes.

DUPLICATING QUIDEL'S NEEDS-BASED APPROACH UNIQUELY IN YOUR INDUSTRY

CREATING A SEGMENTATION HYPOTHESIS FOR FURTHER RESEARCH

Many of our clients would rather save time and turn an entire segmentation approach over to in-house or external market research teams. But with all due respect to the many great market research firms out there, this is the wrong approach.

Like any good scientist, market researchers have to create some kind of hypothesis in order to kick off a segmentation project. Specifically, they need to know what questions to ask customers to define their different needs. They can't just give your customers a blank sheet of paper that says, "Write down what you want."

In our experience, the following hypothesis generation approach leverages the best of both worlds: your team's knowledge of your customers and markets and the ability for market researchers to adjust your hypothesis based on collected data. After all, would you rather create the initial hypothesis, or let your market research firm do it? You may even find that the hypothesis provides enough insight that you don't need to spend a lot more money and time to further validate it.

THE APPROPRIATE MIND-SET: START WITH THE CONCEPT THAT YOU ARE DETERMINING THE DIFFERENCES AMONG GOOD PROSPECTS AND CUSTOMERS

It's important to start the process of creating a segmentation hypothesis by trying to define differences between prospects and customers you'd *like* to do business with, rather than trying to define the differences between good and bad customers.

Companies are much better at defining the characteristics of good versus bad customers than they are at figuring out the differences in needs that desirable customers have. However, the good/bad distinction will focus you in the wrong direction; it will force your attention toward attitudes and behaviors you *would like* customers to exhibit (e.g., not being price sensitive and being easy to serve), rather than on *their motivations and needs*.

(continued)

(continued)

Step 1: Consider Different Segmentation Dimensions Than Your Competitors Do, Like This B2B Marketer Did

We coach many clients to start the segmentation process by brainstorming nonobvious, unique differences between customers. And we've found that they often do not know how to do this or where to begin. The secret lies in using a framework that focuses on customers' varying needs, attitudes, behaviors, and motivations.

The fill-in-the-blank tool shown in Figure 3.2 has proved to be useful in starting the Segmentation Dimension brainstorming process for all types of B2B and B2C companies. This works just as well for companies as it does for consumers. Just imagine that the customer is either an individual or a business, and brainstorm away.

Some customers are trying to accomplish the job of _____ when using products like ours; others are trying to accomplish the job of _____.

Some customers are motivated by_____; others, by_____.

Some customers get their work/tasks done by being _____; others, by being _____.

Some customers approach work/life balance with the attitude of _____; others, with the attitude of _____.

Some customers' environment can be described as _____; others, as _____.

Some customers are inspired by _____; others are inspired by _____.

Some customers have expertise in _____; others have expertise in _____.

Some customers' goals are _____; others' goals are _____.

Some customers' personality styles are _____; others' personality styles are _____.

Some customers' decision-making styles are _____; others' decision-making styles are _____.

Some customers' responsibilities include _____; others' responsibilities include _____.

Some customers' competitive styles can be described as _____; others' can be described as _____.

Figure 3.2　Dimensions of Segmentation Questions, Examples

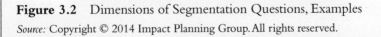

To illustrate, let's look at a company that sold a range of medical administration software products. This company had segmented its markets in exactly the same way its competitors had. These noninsightful segments, classified with names like Large Urban Hospitals and Small Rural Hospitals, provided no clues for identifying and addressing each different hospital segment's motivations and needs.

The software company was intrigued by the concept of needs-based segmentation and decided to update its approach. Unfortunately, the initial efforts were unaided by the type of brainstorming starter list like the one provided in Figure 3.2. As a result, the medical software marketing team fell into their old habit of using descriptive classification when describing differences between their hospital customers:

- Practice type: specialty hospital versus general hospital
- Location: rural hospital versus urban hospital
- Level of influence on other hospitals: high versus low
- Partnership with providers: good partner versus difficult to work with

The process finally got on track when the team used a list like the one shown in Figure 3.2. Specifically, two questions seemed to very clearly describe real differences between good hospital customers:

1. Some hospitals' motivations are being the first to use cutting-edge technology and solutions; others' motivations are ensuring the safety of their patients by using only highly proven solutions.
2. Some hospitals' goals are to maximize their profits; others' goals are to make decisions that provide the best care for patients and let the profits take care of themselves.

Now they were getting somewhere. The team was encouraged to translate these and at least eight or nine additional differences if they could find them, into the binary "this versus that" format introduced in the Quidel story, using the chart shown in Figure 3.3.

(continued)

(*continued*)

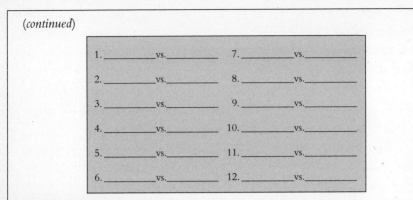

Figure 3.3 Dimensions of Segmentation Template

The team translated the two customer motivations and goals statements they liked into the following binary segmentation dimensions:

Technology adoption: desire to be cutting edge versus desire to use only proven solutions
How they do business: always patient-first emphasis versus strong profit motive

They were ready for the next step.

Step 2: Use Occam's Razor to Choose Dimensions, and Use "Name That Segment" to Create a Hypothesis

Brainstorming can result in several good dimension candidates for your ultimate segmentation hypothesis. Choosing one binary dimension for your hypothesis creates two segments (Quidel's want to be/don't want to be approach), and choosing two binary dimensions for your approach creates four segments, as you will see next. We do not recommend any more than two dimensions/four segments for new segmentation practitioners.

But settling on one to two dimensions from eight to twelve choices (or more!) can be an intimidating task. Which are best? Choosing was easier for the medical software marketer than for most (see following discussion). The company loved a combination of the two binary dimensions described earlier and created the segmentation approach shown in Figure 3.4, complete with names for the four segments.

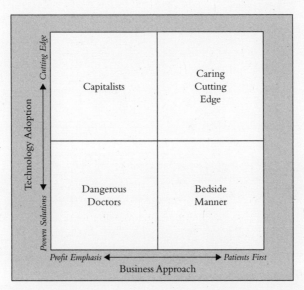

Figure 3.4 Hospital Software Product Needs-Based Segmentation

Hopefully, it's now clear to you how two binary segmentation dimensions create four segments. The company felt that a two-segment model (like Quidel's) was too simplistic for its business; in fact, management already knew and utilized their knowledge of various hospitals' technology adoption profiles. But by combining this dimension with the how they do business dimension, they developed this insightful four-block segmentation that gave immediate clues as to how to create different value propositions and messaging for each.

It's traditionally much harder for teams to choose one or two dimensions from among the 12 or so they come up with. Making this decision often requires experimenting with and examining several combinations of two segmentation dimensions together. Our clients often use the blank templates shown in Figure 3.5 to experiment with several approaches.

(continued)

(continued)

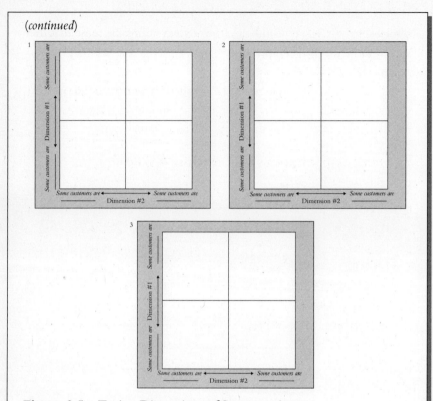

Figure 3.5   Testing Dimensions of Segmentation

Making a final dimension selection and creating a hypothesis is often difficult; however, two ideas can help you out. The first is one that too many people consider to be a throwaway step: naming each potential segment with a combination of creativity and explicitness, like the four-blocker for the hospital software example. This often-fun-but-under-appreciated exercise allows your team to get creative—and typically comes with a great deal of humor.

For example, what would a pharmaceutical company call a segment of doctors whom their reps are trying to engage with, whose primary motivation is to make profits by seeing more patients (not reps), and whose work environments can be described as disorganized and chaotic (not leaving much time for nonpatient business)? Dr. No?

Despite its frequent dismissal, this naming step can be crucial. It often yields a descriptive segment name that immediately draws to mind a specific segment profile and helps give strategy teams the sense that they have found a powerful approach.

The second idea is the previously mentioned Occam's razor approach. When more than one segmentation hypothesis is worth considering, you want to choose the simplest to understand. Simple and powerful works best when it comes to executing segmentation initiatives.

The Final Step: Segmentation Hypothesis Validation

There is one final step that companies can take to convince themselves that they have a viable segmentation hypothesis for further research. *Segmentation validation* builds on the benefits ladder approach from the previous chapter.

Since the purpose of segmentation is to *describe differences between customers,* validation looks at each segment and determines whether they truly do have different needs.

The validation for our hospital marketer shows the output of a benefits ladder (the topic of our previous chapter) down the left hand side and a ranking of each benefit *based on how a company in the segment might prioritize them* (Figure 3.6).

Possible Segments				
Benefits sought	Capitalists	Dangerous Doctors	Caring Cutting Edge	Bedside Manner
Fast Reimbursements	1	2	6	5
Handle More Patients	2	3	3	2
Patient Outcome	4	6	2	1
Ego/Recognition	5	1	5	4
Involved Partnership	6	4	4	3
Latest Technology	3	5	1	6

Figure 3.6   Segmentation Validation Matrix

Source: Copyright © 2014 Impact Planning Group. All rights reserved.

(*continued*)

(continued)

Although many of the benefits may be important to these different segments, *it is the priority* that they place on the benefits that allows us to see if we actually have different segments. As you can see, each of the segments has an entirely different number 1 priority when it comes to benefits sought and an entirely different lowest priority. For example, the Capitalists seek fast reimbursement and handle more patients; they are least likely to want an involved partnership. Clearly, these segments have different needs, allowing us to declare our segmentation plausible and ready for research validation.

At this point, you can hand the segmentation hypothesis over to market research, where it can be adjusted. If you have given the hypothesis process your full attention, you will be surprised how little adjustment will be necessary. And any variations that the research points out will be meaningful, leaving you with an exciting foundation for the rest of your strategic plan.

Segmentation is incredibly powerful—but developing an approach is still an early step in a strategic marketing process. It's tempting to dive right into creating value propositions from here. However, you've got several more important steps to cover first. The next step is to analyze whether all the segments you've defined are worthy of your company's time and resources, which we will do in Chapter 5. However, we'll take a brief detour from segmentation-specific subjects and discuss a very important issue in Chapter 4: your competition!

CHAPTER 4

What Business Are You *Really* In?

How Southwest Fooled Other Airlines into Thinking They Were the Competition

POWER TOOLS: MARKET TREE AND COMPETITOR ANALYSIS

Those skilled at making the enemy move do so by creating a situation to which he must conform; they entice him with something he is certain to take, and with lures of ostensible profit they await him in strength.

> —Sun Tzu, Chinese military general, strategist,
> and philosopher, from *The Art of War*

MOST COMPANIES ARE TOO FLIPPANT WHEN DEFINING THEIR COMPETITIVE ENVIRONMENT

You can't blame a marketer for wanting certain parts of a strategic plan to be easy to concoct. After all, creating tactics for staying one step ahead of your presumed competitors is enough work. Describing the market in which you are competing—and the specific competitors you are facing—should take only about 5 minutes, right? Isn't this just a throwaway step before you get to the *real* strategic work?

Not so fast. The ability to define your market broadly and creatively can be a source of competitive advantage, as this chapter's cases will prove. You can jump-start the very process most marketers want to get to—*finding ideas to beat the competitors*—by uncovering some insights around the very basic question "What business are you *really* in?"

But finding new ways to define your market can't be the end game. After you take this step, you must wisely choose a battleground, one that leverages your company's capabilities to meet more customer needs than competitors do.

This chapter features the story of Southwest Airlines to illustrate how all these factors can work together. As with some of the other companies we discuss in this book, Southwest's story, strategies, and tactics have been well publicized. But it's a lesser-known aspect of Southwest's strategy that is the primary secret to its success.

You'll see how Southwest defined its market in a way that gave it a perspective on its opportunities that differed from their competitors'. You'll also learn how this perspective allowed Southwest to make seemingly prescient strategic decisions, while competitors made exactly the wrong choices, leading to radically different business results for each. After reading Southwest's story, you'll come to appreciate the importance of defining markets—and competitors—*from your customers' perspective.*

At the end of this chapter, we'll show you some market scoping and competitor identification tools that will demonstrate that you have more options than you thought you did. You'll see how the seemingly simple process of defining your markets and competitors can become a source of innovation that leads to profitable growth.

LUV-ERS, NOT FIGHTERS

Southwest Airlines' turbulent early days should have spawned the type of company that attacks competitors head-on. It would be easy to attribute Southwest's business success to ruthless (albeit quirky and fun) directly competitive tactics that drive fares down and weak airlines out of business.

For more misleading evidence that Southwest is a merciless competitor itching for its next fight, just look at the picture on the cover of the best-selling book about Southwest titled *Nuts!,* written by Kevin and Jackie Freiberg in 1996. There you'll find a picture of Southwest cofounder and former chief executive officer (CEO), Herb Kelleher—who once arm-wrestled another airline executive to settle a lawsuit—with his sleeves rolled up, tattooed arms showing, and near-snarl on his face as he throws a bag of peanuts toward the camera.

You wouldn't expect a company that is, by all accounts, a reflection of Kelleher's personality to be crafty Luv-ers (LUV is the company's stock symbol, reflecting its passion for their business) instead of bare-knuckle brawlers. But looking more deeply into Southwest's story reveals a little-known secret.

After facing down some direct competitor airlines in its early days, Southwest set its sights on a different type of competitor than most would guess. Along the way, the Southwest team revealed some strategies that all companies can learn from when defining their markets.

AT FIRST, A GOOD OLD-FASHIONED, TEXAS-SIZED BARROOM BRAWL

As recounted in Kevin and Jackie Freiberg's great account of Southwest's story in *Nuts! Southwest Airlines' Crazy Recipe for Business and Personal Success,* the airline's initial difficulties getting its business off the ground reads like an overdone drama. Smug, fat-cat competitors in a highly regulated airline industry plied tactics against the upstart company that—one would think—could never fly in the real world. But it was Texas in the late 1960s, and these things really happened.

Incumbents Braniff Airways and Texas International (TI) just didn't want another competitor, even if the fledgling Southwest's early intentions were simply to fly between Dallas, Houston, and San Antonio. The Texas Aeronautics Commission (TAC) quickly approved Southwest's application for intrastate travel, but Braniff and TI filed a restraining order, arguing that Texas didn't need another airline.

Although Kelleher, an attorney by trade, proved to be an incredibly effective court fighter, the legal battles took a toll. Southwest prevailed with the Civil Aeronautics Board (CAB), but at a huge cost. At one point, the company had $142 in the bank and more than $80,000 in overdue bills. Heroic efforts by Lamar Muse, at the time a Southwest executive, to procure $750,000 from an angel investor kept things going.

Two days before Southwest's initial flight, Braniff and TI somehow obtained another restraining order to keep the new airline from launching.

Thanks to Kelleher's deft legal maneuvering, the Texas Supreme Court threw out the restraining order. The very next day, on June 18, 1971, Southwest Airlines was operating flights, having fought off challenges that would have killed lesser-willed companies.

Several years later, Braniff and TI faced the consequences of their overbearing efforts. Both pleaded no contest when a federal court indicted them under the Sherman Antitrust Act for their actions to keep Southwest from starting up. However, the $100,000 in fines that both were forced to pay seems paltry in comparison to what it put the young airline through.

Southwest was finally free to fly, and despite some other early challenges, it went on to become a great business success story. Given this early history, it's not surprising to see quotes like this one from Colleen Barret, Southwest's legal secretary at the time: "The warrior mentality, the very fight to survive, was what created our culture" (quoted from *Nuts!*, page 27).

Yet despite Barret's quote, many of Southwest's strategic actions seem to be more in line with those of a general who has seen war and tries to find other, less violent ways to achieve objectives.

SOUTHWEST COULD HAVE MADE THE SAME FATAL MARKET DEFINITION DECISIONS THAT PEOPLE EXPRESS MADE

All enterprises have to define the business that they are in, if only for purposes of tax reporting laws. But very successful businesses see the wisdom in working hard at it.

They examine different ways to define the markets in which they compete and commonly are working in a very different paradigm than competitors. This often allows them to see more and different opportunities than competitors do.

To illustrate, we will bring a Southwest-like competitor into our story, an airline that started well but died far too soon. The now-defunct People Express had a fast start back in the early 1980s, but the pressure the company felt to grow led management to make some fatal decisions. They took some paths that Southwest has managed to avoid. The two airlines' different results are largely a function of taking radically different approaches to answering the question, "What business are we *really* in?"

A TALE OF TWO "FOR THE PEOPLE" AIRLINES—ONE DOESN'T END WELL

You can assume a great deal about People Express's early focus from its name. The airline was founded in 1981 with a low-cost "for the people" business model. Its original service featured no-frills, low-cost flying from Newark, New Jersey, to just three cities: Buffalo, New York; Columbus, Ohio; and Norfolk, Virginia.

Its early success earned the company some flattering comparisons to Southwest, with predictions of People Express's expansion creating a Midwest/East equivalent to its southern competitor. Six years later, People Express was bankrupt and ceased to exist. What happened?

An accounting of some of the main events on the path to People Express's demise is instructive. Contrast it to a similar accounting of some of Southwest's key milestones, depicted in Figure 4.1.

People Express	Southwest
• Added 747s in 1983 and began flying to London	• Begins service outside of Texas in 1980, flying to New Orleans, 7 full years after its inaugural flight in 1973 (remember, People Express lasted only 6 Years!)
• Added premium-class seats	
• Acquired Frontier Airlines in 1985 and became the fifth biggest U.S. carrier	• Expands service to California in 1982—11 years after inception
• Began creaking under huge debt and integration problems in 1986; increased prices	• Begins service at Chicago's Midway Airport—instead of the much larger O'Hare—in 1985
• Added first-class seats for international travel	• Annual revenue passed $1 billion in 1989
• Became full service, competing with American, United, British Airways, etc.	• Expands to the East Coast in 1993—22 years after inception—with service at Baltimore-Washington Airport
• Forced into fire sale and sold assets to Continental	
• Ceased to exist in February 1987, after only 6 years of operation	• Begins service at Long Island MacArthur Airport but avoids more congested, larger New York City airports in 1999

Figure 4.1 Timelines of People Express and Southwest

What do you notice while looking at these timelines? It's tempting to say that the lessons learned range from grow slowly and stick to the knitting when it comes to success in the airline business.

THE STORY OF PEOPLE EXPRESS SHOWS THE DANGERS OF A TOO-SIMPLISTIC MARKET DEFINITION

But these easy conclusions miss some much bigger points. For one, let's look at how defining their markets played a huge role in the extremely different results each company achieved.

A company's strategies flow directly from *how it defines itself.* Southwest and People Express initially defined their markets similarly, but at some point, both began viewing themselves *very* differently.

Using a simple tool we call a market tree, it's easy to imagine the companies' market definitions looked like Figure 4.2.

The danger—and where we think the two airlines took dissimilar paths in their market definitions—is when companies start to feel pressure to grow. This is the time that companies typically revisit their earlier market definition decisions and look for new opportunities. During this reassessment, a company must:

- Consider alternative market definition approaches, *and*
- Have a fundamental understanding of its own core capabilities.

Violating one or both of these principles can be a recipe for disaster. And it was mistakes in these two areas that sealed People Express's demise. As the company looked to grow, it assumed that the higher-cost travel market was the next logical target.

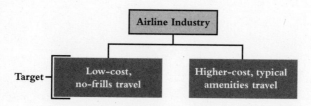

Figure 4.2   People Express's and Southwest's Early-Stage Market Definition

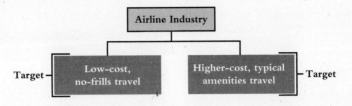

Figure 4.3 People Express's Next-Stage Market Definition

Its early success likely led to overconfidence in attacking new, different markets such as international travel ("This company can do anything it puts its mind to") when it should have been looking for ways to grow that built on its core capabilities as a low-cost carrier (Figure 4.3).

How did Southwest avoid these traps when it faced the pressure to grow business? For starters, it moved from the initial, simple, start-up market definition to one that looked at its markets more broadly.

HOW TO DEFINE YOUR MARKET MORE *BROADLY*, LIKE GE DOES

Perhaps Southwest took a page from General Electric's (GE's) book when defining its market more broadly. During his reign, famous ex-GE CEO Jack Welch became frustrated when seeing extremely narrow market definitions from his business units. They were trying to comply with Jack's mandate that every GE business be number 1 or number 2 in their market—or be closed or sold.

As a hypothetical example, if a van and truck vehicle leasing business *could* define their market as "the van and truck leasing market" but had poor share in van leasing, they *would* define their business more tightly as "the truck leasing market."

"We fixed many GE units' overly tight market definitions by saying that businesses had to define their market in such a way that their share of any market they were in could not be more than 10 percent. That restriction forced people into a whole new mind-set, and opportunities for growth were suddenly everywhere," Welch wrote in *Winning* (page 174).

Welch's idea provides a good way to more *broadly* define a maturing market: find a way to define the market wider such that your share is less than 10 percent.

We know of a company that was making disposable leads—the connections at the end of the wires that stick to one's body when undergoing an electro-cardiogram (ECG) or other similar medical procedure.

This company thought it was in the disposable leads business. Market share was stagnant. However, management realized that some new microchip tech-nologies that they could easily source would make their leads smart, send-ing important patient data to central nursing stations that previously required hands-on nursing attention. The company began defining its broader market as the patient monitoring business. A whole host of new growth opportunities emerged from this redefining of its market.

A word of caution: jumping into a more broadly defined market is not always a good idea. People Express's foray into international travel is a clear example of this. Disaster can ensue when a company attempts to compete in a broader market without having core capabilities suited for it.

In a moment we'll see how Southwest created a broader market defi-nition in a way that truly leveraged its core capabilities. But first, let's look at another way to find useful market definitions that open up new opportunities.

HOW TO USE *CUSTOMER-CENTRIC* COMPETITOR IDENTIFICATION FOR *CREATIVE* MARKET DEFINITIONS

Sometimes, especially in developing or newer markets, merely thinking more broadly won't generate enough new market definition options. In these cases, finding ways to define markets more *creatively* adds fuel to the fire.

A process simply called *Competitor Identification* leads to new market defini-tion possibilities. It starts with listing all the competitors a company can think of, aided by a couple of key definitions:

Direct competitors are defined as "companies in the same market with the same or similar product or process technologies." These are head-to-head, apples-to-apples competitors. Keeping with our chapter theme, this describes the competition between Southwest and Delta, United, American, and the like. Many companies tend to think *only* of direct competitors when they speak of their enemies. But it's important to list them all—and then turn your thinking to a different kind of competitor.

DIRECT COMPETITORS CAN HURT YOU, BUT INDIRECT COMPETITORS CAN KILL YOU

Indirect competitors are often much more dangerous than direct ones. Indirect competitors are companies that "compete in the same market with products that serve the same customer function or benefit . . . but do this using different product or process technologies."

For example, a new breed of dogs is entering the medical diagnostics market that can detect cancer with a high degree of accuracy in humans simply by smelling their breath. The dogs serve the same function as the computed tomography (CT) scans but use a different process. This surprised a manufacturer of expensive CT scan devices and sent them scurrying to figure out ways to address this new indirect competitor.

At the same time, a more nimble company was applying the science of dog's keen sense of smell. Metabolomx developed a personal computer–based system with a hose attached. According to the company, the system analyzes the breath and its volatile complex components (VOCs). Tumors produce their own VOCs. As stated on its website, Metabolomx is in the business of diagnosing disease based on the signature pattern of metabolic biomarkers in breath.

Another example of indirect competition is in credit cards. Although Visa, MasterCard, and American Express were working hard to take market share and customers from one another, an indirect competitor has emerged: paying for things through a phone. It serves the same basic benefits . . . plus it is more functional.

Companies can be blindsided—even put out of business—by indirect competitors, because they don't see them coming. But it is also important to identify all direct and indirect competitors for another important, less scary reason: indirect competitor identification can give you ideas for how to more creatively define your market.

INDIRECTS CAN STAY HIDDEN FROM VIEW UNLESS YOU TALK TO CUSTOMERS

Is the CT scan company mentioned earlier in the CT scan business—or the disease detection business? If it had defined itself as disease-detectors, would it have been more creative in its thinking and perhaps not been so surprised by the cancer-sniffing dogs?

Companies can make sure they identify *all* indirect competitors by asking customers: "What are all the options you consider when considering a product or service like ours?" They can then ask themselves internally: "If *that's* who our competitor is, what business are we *really* in?"

Leveraging a combination of Jack Welch's approach and competitor identification, companies can consider several alternatives for defining their markets broadly and creatively. But they must also choose *where* they will compete intelligently. As we return to the chapter's primary story, it seems clear that Southwest used this total approach brilliantly.

SOUTHWEST'S BROAD, CREATIVE, AND INTELLIGENT MARKET DEFINITION SECRET

How did Southwest define its market differently enough that it made many of the *same successful* strategies discussed here *unsuccessful* for their direct competitors?

- Serving nuts and a soft drink on Southwest's short flights, largely without complaint, while other airlines are relentlessly criticized for their lack of culinary taste.
- Boarding planes in an egalitarian, first-come, first-serve manner that customers readily accept, while other airlines have to cater to million-miler fliers who want to board first.
- Thriving while staying away from a typical hub-and-spoke system to reduce delays and maximize time in the air, while other airlines have to provide service just about everywhere to engender loyalty.
- Utilizing all of these strategies, and more, to keep airline fares at such a low level that other airlines still fight to keep them out of new markets.

The answer is, they didn't view themselves as competitors of other airlines!

When a Southwest shareholder asked Herb Kelleher in the early days why, in a situation where they had a significant pricing advantage over a competitor, they couldn't "raise our prices just two or three dollars," Herb replied, "You don't understand. We aren't competing with other airlines; we're *competing with ground transportation*" (emphasis added; quote from page 54 of *Nuts!*).

LIKE SUN TZU'S QUOTE, SOUTHWEST LURES COMPETITORS TO FIGHT A WAR THEY CAN'T WIN

There it is: the clue that's often missed that defines a huge part of Southwest's success. When facing pressure to grow, Southwest revisited its simple, early-stage market definition. And instead of looking at other airlines as competitors—and dangerously expanding scope like People Express did— Southwest targeted a different, indirect competitor than their early battles would suggest (Figure 4.4).

By having a broader, more creative view of the market than People Express did and having a firmer understanding of its core capabilities, Southwest had radically different results.

Southwest understood that, as an operationally excellent airline, its expertise allowed them to target a market space that would invite huge growth. By creating a strong, no-frills value proposition, people began to consider air rather than road travel. In addition, by making a clear choice, customers know what Southwest stands for and understand that the airline's frugal ways benefit them via lower fares—and not having to drive!

Many competitor airlines would argue that Southwest *was* targeting them. Certainly, many of them have been lured into dangerously lowering fares and trying to duplicate Southwest's approaches to their demise.

But the contrast with the People Express method—and that of many other businesses like them who expanded their market definition without thinking or waded into a battle they shouldn't have fought in the first place—shows that Southwest was playing from an entirely different sheet of music. It utilized to

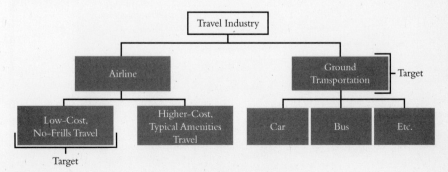

Figure 4.4   Southwest's Next-Stage Market Definition

Source: Copyright © 2014 Impact Planning Group. All rights reserved.

perfection a market definition process that broadly and creatively defined its market, but did so in a way that also played to its unique strengths. Sun Tzu, whose quote is featured at the start of this chapter, would approve.

DUPLICATING SOUTHWEST'S MARKET-DEFINING INSIGHTS UNIQUELY IN YOUR INDUSTRY

MARKET TREE AND COMPETITOR IDENTIFICATION TOOLS

The two very simple tools featured earlier in this chapter will help you think broadly and creatively when defining your market: The Market Tree tool helps companies define their market, and the Competitor Identification tool will highlight direct and indirect competitors and help refine a Market Tree while determining whether it is too simplistic.

THE MARKET TREE FORMAT WILL GET YOU STARTED

The format discussed here kicks off the market definition process. Although straightforward, it will often spur some useful and even insightful debate. On its own, this may lead to choosing a more fitting target for a company than it had before.

Figure 4.5 is how Southwest's initial market tree might have looked. The dollar signs represent the available revenue in each component of

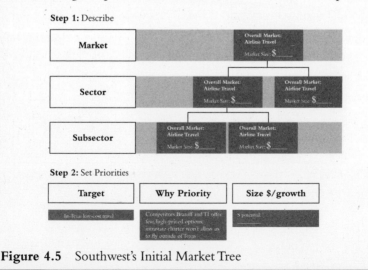

Figure 4.5 Southwest's Initial Market Tree

the Market Tree. Although we have left these blank because the data from that time period are not readily available, this is important information to include in *your* Market Tree.

However, as People Express found out, there are risks in defining a market too simply. For this reason, we recommend two more actions before setting final priorities:

1. *Expand.* Try a modified form of the Jack Welch rule and see if it helps: ask, "How would we define our market more broadly, to have much *less* market share than we have in our current definition?"

2. *Get creative.* Use the Competitor Identification tool that follows to see if this gives you more ideas for creative ways to define your market.

DEFINING COMPETITORS FROM A CUSTOMER STANDPOINT WILL ENHANCE YOUR MARKET DEFINITION APPROACH

The Competitor Identification template that follows has one simple rule: don't forget anyone! The definitions in the Southwest story make clear what direct and indirect competitors are.

On the tool's *y*-axis, *Actual* refers to companies that compete with a company now. *Potential* are those that *could* compete in the future.

Complementers are companies that call on the same customers as a particular company but sell different, noncompetitive, complementary things. A classic example of this is how peanuts and other salty snacks are great complementers to beer. Complementers can quickly become significant competitors.

In total, the Competitor Identification tool should lead a company to ask, "If these are our competitors and complementers, what market or business are we really in?"

Figure 4.6 shows how Southwest may have looked at its competitive landscape as it began to look for ways to grow.

(continued)

(*continued*)

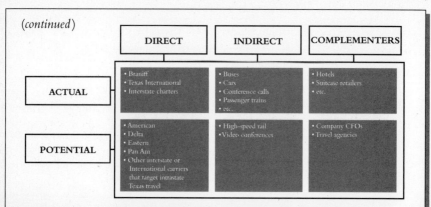

Figure 4.6   Southwest's Competitor Identification
Source: Copyright © 2014 Impact Planning Group. All rights reserved.

Key point: This information is best sourced from asking potential customers what *they consider* all of their options in a product category to be.

REFINING A MARKET TREE BASED ON JACK WELCH AND COMPETITOR IDENTIFICATION

Applying the Jack Welch rule and completing the Competitor Identification tool will lead you to refine an initial Market Tree. One can imagine Southwest using both approaches and asking the question: "If buses, cars, and trains are our competitors, what business are we really in?" The answer led to the targeting decision that is the basis for this chapter—and Southwest's success (Figure 4.7).

GUIDELINES FOR CHOOSING A TARGET

So, how do companies make a good targeting choice and ultimately decide what business they *really* are in? The lesson from Southwest is clear: when defining your company's market, think broadly and creatively. Consider your expanded set of direct and indirect competitors. Then choose your definition based on your company's unique core competencies. (You'll find even more help on this in Chapter 6 with our Ability to Win tool.)

People Express tried to enter a market—long distance, international travel—that required different skills than it had as a low-cost airline. The misguided effort failed miserably and killed the company.

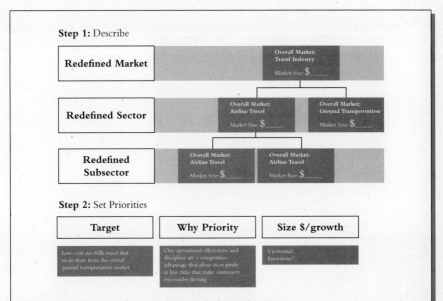

Step 1: Describe

Figure 4.7   Southwest's Expanded Market Tree

On the other hand, Southwest knew that its operational skills could make it an attractive option to ground transportation. So its expanded market definition had the opposite result.

WHAT'S NEXT?

Because defining a market is an early-stage step in a strategic marketing process, it's important to have a working market definition hypothesis at the start. Make the best choice you can for now.

The stories, tools, and frameworks in the subsequent chapters of this book will help you continually refine your market definition hypothesis. Stay tuned, and don't forget to revisit your choices here often as you go through your strategic plan process!

CHAPTER 5

Who Do You Love?

How Enterprise Picked Up the Number 1 Market Share in Rental Cars

POWER TOOL: SEGMENT ATTRACTIVENESS

Life is what happens when you are busy making other plans
> —John Lennon, English musician, singer, and songwriter

HOW TO ELIMINATE DISTRACTION AND STAY FOCUSED ON PLAYING WHERE YOU CAN WIN BIG

Want to win a bet? Ask anyone who's not in the travel business to name the top rental car company in the United States. Nine out of 10 will guess—incorrectly—that the answer is Hertz or Avis.

The undisputed number 1, whether your criteria are number of cars, number of locations, or revenue is . . . drumroll please . . . Enterprise. And it's not even a close race; Enterprise at least *doubles* the results of its closest competitor, Hertz, in these categories.

Those who are familiar with Enterprise associate the company with legendary customer service and the memorable "We'll Pick You Up" advertising campaign that was originally launched in the 1980s and is still used today. But there is another, lesser known aspect of Enterprise's approach that reveals a secret to its success.

For more than 30 years, Enterprise expertly chose a target—while ignoring other, bigger opportunities—and focused *all* of its resources on this segment of customers. We call the process of selecting a target *Segment Attractiveness Analysis,* an approach that any organization *can* duplicate and benefit from relatively easily and quickly. However, most don't.

The reason that the vast majority of companies don't target well is because they are afraid of missing opportunities. They think that the entire market is their target. And although it's not realistic to suggest that all companies should focus on one segment only, it is our experience that marshaling significant resources toward one or a few segments is *vastly superior* to diluting efforts across a too-wide playing field. In other words, you cannot be everything to everyone. You *must* have a focus.

Some companies start out focused but prematurely expand their range of targets. This causes them to miss chances to reach the growth goals they've set through segment domination and market expansion. Still others hesitate to explicitly define a target, because they believe in letting managers and salespeople decide what a good opportunity looks like.

If you never take the time to target with specificity and discipline, you waste tremendous time and resources chasing unprofitable opportunities. Conversely, Enterprise's focus led it to fully leverage the company's core capabilities.

This chapter will break down Enterprise's path to a world-class targeting strategy. We'll see how its ability to concentrate on a specific target segment uncovered opportunities, strategies, and partnerships that its competitors completely missed until it was too late.

The Segment Attractiveness analysis tool that we'll review at the end of this chapter provides an instrument for alignment that spells out the steps to making targets clear and identifiable. This tool will make sure that your entire organization is aligned and aware of the opportunities that leverage your company's capabilities to the fullest.

THE ACCIDENTAL RENTAL CAR COMPANY

As recounted in Kirk Kazanjian's engaging, detailed account of Enterprise's history, *Exceeding Customer Expectations,* Jack Taylor didn't like the idea of renting cars. The legendary Enterprise founder was running his 1950s start-up as a car leasing company, a concept that was much better suited to the type of world-class customer service he fervently believed in than was renting cars.

His passion for service was a result of his post–World War II work in the automobile sales industry. Jack loved dealing with people and opposed the many heavy-handed, customer-alienating tactics that, unfortunately, still exist in the automobile sales business today.

He started a leasing company because, in his mind, leasing was all about customer relationships. What could be better for customers than getting to drive a new car every couple of years (the term of a typical lease contract), thus avoiding many of the maintenance issues that owning older cars bring? And when a lease contract expires, the customer returns it to the dealership with the intentions of leasing another car.

Jack saw an opportunity to ditch the short-term tactics in car sales and create the type of long-term relationships, lease after lease, that he instinctively knew were good for business. This was how he was going to build his company.

But destiny seemed to have other plans for Jack and his fledgling firm. Sporadically at first, but with increasing frequency, leasing customers began asking to . . . gasp . . . *rent cars!*

Jack considered renting to be leasing's far less attractive cousin. For one, it seemed to require a mass-marketing approach that was the antithesis of Jack's desires for intimate, long-term, one-to-one customer relationships.

But as much as he disparaged renting, Jack didn't like to disappoint his customers. He showed a willingness to experiment by making a few exceptions and renting out some of his idle lease vehicles—and nothing terrible happened. In fact, renting allowed the branches to gain some revenue from the inactive cars in their fleet.

Then, as word spread that Jack's company, called Enterprise, was renting cars, business began to pick up. Jack, showing a flexibility that is uncommon among early-stage entrepreneurs, began *reconsidering* his original business plan.

Over a weekend, Jack made a decision that eventually would alter the balance of power in a multibillion dollar rental car industry: if Enterprise was going to rent cars, they were going to "do it right." Jack instructed one of his managers to come up with the number of cars the company should buy and earmark for its rental fleet.

This quiet first step launched a series of brilliant strategic moves—which we will cover in the ensuing pages—that led Enterprise to tremendous growth, ultimately toppling Hertz, Avis, and other rental car industry players. The formula for Enterprise's success included:

- Defining an *underserved segment* in a maturing industry
- *Forging relationships* with a seemingly obvious stakeholder *untapped* by Enterprise's competitors

- Implementing an *agency location strategy* that created barriers to competitors entering the business
- Executing a successful customer service strategy by *getting the right customers into their agencies in the first place*

Enterprise did all of this under the radar of its bigger rivals. Management worked unnoticed until it was too late for any of the incumbents to do anything to counter their momentum.

As we dig into the details of Enterprise's strategies, you'll see how targeting was the key to its success. The company stayed focused on serving a specific segment while virtually every one of its competitors was vying for business in a different, but much bigger segment.

THE KEY TO LONG-TERM SUCCESS: FLEXIBILITY IN THE EARLY DAYS, DISCIPLINE AS YOU INVEST FOR GROWTH

Great targeting starts with great segmentation and market definition, which we discussed in Chapters 3 and 4. From the story of Southwest Airlines, we learned that a company must first be aware of the different ways it can define its alternatives.

Like Southwest, Enterprise was forced in its early days to think about alternatives for defining its *market*. Although it had clearly identified its market as leasing, its customers were asking it to consider being in the rental car market.

As the Enterprise team thought about its alternatives, they probably would have drawn the simple automobile market segmentation diagram shown in Figure 5.1.

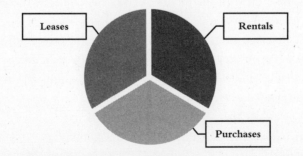

Figure 5.1 Automobile Market Segmentation

How did Enterprise decide to respond to these rental car requests? It quickly decided to shift focus and put significant resources into renting cars.

Wait a minute . . . isn't this story about targeting, focus, and discipline? Yes, but there is a counterintuitive approach that can help companies decide when to be flexible and when to be focused.

Many *successful* start-ups *changed* their original business plan largely based on customer feedback. In fact, flexibility is often necessary for survival in the early stages of a company's growth.

Prudently altering course—before committing huge sums of capital to build a business around the wrong opportunity—is a key to many eventually successful companies' ability to make it at the beginning. Conversely, many start-ups die because they lack the kind of early-stage flexibility that Jack Taylor demonstrated.

But here's the other side of the coin: once a company has moved beyond the start-up phase, it begins investing heavily in infrastructure to serve a target. If these investments have successfully created strong core competencies and certain advantages for its target customer, then it is time to stay focused.

Many established businesses flounder because they are *too willing* to continually expand or change focus at this more mature stage and never leverage the advantages that they have invested heavily to create. In other words, timing is absolutely crucial.

Even though these maturing businesses have the kind of established capabilities that they *could* apply in a differentiated manner with the right target and focus, they instead chase every opportunity. And they end up at a disadvantage in both arenas: they aren't able to offer anything unique or build any kind of lasting competitive advantage.

Enterprise flexibly considered the rental car market, but then built out its infrastructure, partnerships, and strategies with discipline. The team's focus was immensely aided by an early discovery that emerged soon after Enterprise entered the rental car market seriously. Much like the story of Quidel in our previous chapter, Enterprise uncovered an *unnoticed customer* segment.

ENTERPRISE MOVED BEYOND MARKET SEGMENTATION TO CUSTOMER SEGMENTATION

Ask a business team how they segment their market, and they are likely to show you an approach like the automobile market segmentation shown in

Figure 5.1. But ask them how they segment their *customers,* and you are likely to get a blank stare. That's because it's typical to think that the process of segmentation is completed when they do it at the market level.

As we saw with Quidel in Chapter 3, having a better understanding than your competitors do of how segments of customers might use different products *differently* is an enormous advantage. And when you target segments that competitors *don't know exist,* you can build a value proposition with different components to serve these different needs, thus truly differentiating your company's offer.

At the time that Enterprise entered the rental car market, the accepted target customer for virtually all of the industry players was the travel segment. This consisted of people who were renting cars away from where they lived for business or vacation travel.

Because they listened to the *reasons* leasing customers cited when asking for rental cars, Enterprise's managers were hearing of a *completely different* set of needs. Taylor's customers wanted a rental when their car was in the shop for repairs or when an extra car was needed for trips close to home, such as weekend getaways or when relatives were visiting.

Jack Taylor and his team knew that that they had discovered something extremely valuable: an unnoticed, underserved *customer segment* within the *rental car market segment.* Enterprise called these customers the home market segment (Figure 5.2).

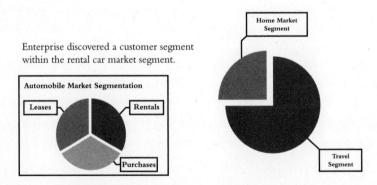

Figure 5.2   Rental Car Market Customer Segmentation

Would focusing here support Enterprise's long-term growth? Or would the company eventually have to compete in the bigger travel segment in order to grow—and compete with companies that had a big head start and advantage?

Enterprise knew it needed further analysis. But there were some good signs that the home market could give Enterprise an edge against competitors.

THE HOME MARKET SEGMENT HAD A MORE DESIRABLE RENTAL CAR RISK PROFILE

One of those good signs was the risk profile of the home market segment. Compared with the travel segment, the home market segment was found to be a pretty good bet from the beginning. Many of Enterprise's first home market renters were also leasing customers: affluent, financially astute individuals whose leasing contracts incented them to take good care of their cars.

This was also a nice profile for a renter. But would these traits hold as the company's growth exposed them to more and more segment customers?

As word got out that Enterprise was renting cars, there was a subtle-yet-growing change to this profile, which led the company to worry even more about managing risk. Would Enterprise's insistence on renting to only good risks in what seemed to be a smaller segment cause the company to run out of good opportunities?

One has to assume that internal debate simmered continuously: Was it time yet to enter the competition for the travel segment?

Fortunately for Enterprise's long-term success, the management team's consensus at the time was, "Not yet." Instead of entering the travel segment, Enterprise uncovered a creative new way to grow the business—in fact, the entire segment—while holding onto its financial discipline and home market focus. It all started with a chance visit to an old friend by an Enterprise employee playing a hunch.

THE DISCOVERY OF A POWERFUL, HIDDEN STAKEHOLDER LOCKS ENTERPRISE'S FOCUS INTO PLACE

On the way back to the Orlando office after a routine visit to a corporate customer, an ambitious Enterprise corporate sales manager had a spontaneous thought: Why not visit an automobile insurance executive he knew and check out an idea for a potential partnership between the insurer and the rental car firm? The premise for the visit was that a significant insurance law—one that insurance companies were lamenting—was about to go into effect. The Enterprise sales manager had a potential win-win-win idea.

The impending Florida law would require insurers to provide reimbursement to customers involved in accidents more quickly. If the contract provided for it, this included immediate authorization of a rental if the insured's car was inoperable. Before this change, insurers were permitted to wait until fault was assessed in an accident before authorizing any type of reimbursement.

So the Enterprise employee made the following pitch: If this change was inevitable, why shouldn't an insurer embrace it and gain a competitive advantage by having a *ready-made relationship* with a rental car company? This type of arrangement could streamline the administrative hassles associated with getting a replacement or loaner car, making a stressful situation less so.

In fact, he explained, forging such a relationship with Enterprise specifically would be great for business. With its rapidly growing, well-deserved reputation for outstanding customer service, the rental transaction could be a rose in the thorn of continual frustration that is typically a part of being involved in a car accident.

The concept was worth a test, and the insurance company agreed to a partnership. The program execution was flawless, consistent with Enterprise's passion for customer service excellence, and the initiative was a big success. Soon Enterprise was duplicating this type of relationship all over the country. Even reputable body shops were added to this growing partnership network.

As the partnership program gained momentum, Enterprise realized several unintended, fortuitous benefits. It benefited from a new customer acquisition standpoint because the insurance companies and body shops referred customers to the firm constantly. The resulting stream of new renters was a big reason that Enterprise was able to grow so stealthily and sneak up on its competitors. These partner referrals reduced the need for mass-market advertising.

In addition, the experience that the insurers' customers had with Enterprise created goodwill for all parties. This encouraged the insurers to expand the number of contracts they wrote that included rental car coverage. This grew the home market segment. By 2004, *Auto Rental News* was reporting that the home market had actually surpassed what it called the airport market in car rental revenues.

Just as important, the insurance company partnerships ultimately elim-inated Enterprise's concerns about having to relax its credit standards in order to achieve growth and scale. It no longer had to worry that certain home market segment renters would be able to pay, because they knew that *the renters themselves* weren't the ones guaranteeing the payment. The big, financially conservative insurance companies were the credit risk in the transaction.

After many years of incredible growth fueled by these insurance company partnerships, Enterprise once again wrestled with the prospects of entering the travel segment to support its goals for growth. But this time, as a larger, via-ble rental car company in its own right, the discussions about expanding focus were more defensive in nature: What if Hertz or Avis recognized what a great business renting to the home market segment was and started eating away at Enterprise's market?

Just as the company began to think about protecting its turf, Enterprise realized how its focus had actually *already* created a powerful barrier to its still larger competitors.

ENTERPRISE'S TARGETING CREATES MASSIVE BARRIERS TO ENTRY TO THE HOME MARKET SEGMENT

There is nothing more unusual in business—in *any* industry—than an uncon-tested market. Find an untapped opportunity, and you can be sure that soon there will be plenty of competition. So perhaps the most unusual aspect of the Enterprise story is that the company is *still,* to this day, the only national or global rental car company that seriously competes for the business of the more than $10 billion home market segment. How can that be?

As the company's focus on the home market segment drove huge growth through the 1970s, it found itself with offices in very different places than the airport-centric locations of Hertz and Avis. Given its roots in the leasing busi-ness, Enterprise's initial locations were often near car dealerships, urban city centers, and growing suburban strip malls.

Its partnerships with insurance companies and auto body shops spurred more of these types of locations. Just as the company began to anticipate home market segment competition from the rental car giants, it began to realize that these *locations* were a huge advantage, because in most cases, Enterprise was much closer to its home market customers than competitors' airport locations! Who wanted to have to go all the way to the airport to get a replacement rental car after having an auto accident?

Today, there is an Enterprise branch within 15 miles of 90 percent of the U.S. population. The lack of competition in the home market segment likely meant that potential competitors soon realized that their existing infrastructure wouldn't cut it. They had to acknowledge that they would need to make massive investments in locations closer to where the segment lived in order to compete with Enterprise. Had Enterprise deviated from its home market focus too soon and begun competing in the travel segment by investing in airport locations, it would not have built this significant barrier to entry.

It was these locations that were the catalyst for Enterprise's next wave of growth: its foray into mass-market advertising to reach more of the home market segment.

"WE'LL PICK YOU UP" WORKED BECAUSE NO COMPETITOR COULD ECONOMICALLY MATCH IT

Enterprise's highly successful "We'll Pick You Up" campaign of the 1980s helped the company reach its next level of growth. After years of relying on partnerships and word of mouth to gain new customers, these television commercials sought to reach new customers via the airwaves. The campaign featured a big promise: Enterprise offered to pick renters up at their home or business and drive them to the agency location. The home market renter—especially the ones with cars in the shop—appreciated this greatly.

The campaign did more than introduce a whole new wave of home market renters to the company. It served to really differentiate Enterprise for a reason directly related to its focus-driven location strategy: *no other competitor could economically match Enterprise's service.* The airport-based locations of Hertz, Avis, and others were just too far away from the typical home market renter.

TARGETING ENABLES A LEGENDARY CUSTOMER SERVICE STRATEGY

A final reason for Enterprise's massive growth is its historically high rate of *repeat business.* Enterprise has become legendary for its customer service excellence and the loyalty it engenders.

The company is one of the few that puts its business practices where its money is when it comes to customer satisfaction. It does so by tying incentives and promotions to managers' ability to deliver high survey scores via a simple, powerful customer satisfaction survey.

But could Enterprise's targeting and focus be another big reason for its tremendous customer loyalty? Consider this finding: a phenomenon called the service recovery paradox suggests that customers who have had a previous problem or issue with a company that was satisfactorily resolved are *more loyal than customers who have never had a problem at all.* So what does this have to do with Enterprise and its focus discipline?

Enterprise's insurance company partnerships brought in customers who had recently experienced one of life's most stressful situations: an automobile accident. The company delivered relief to stranded customers with customer service excellence—and no doubt got extra emotional credit for their efforts. Maybe Enterprise wouldn't have gained the same extra credit operating in the less stressful travel segment.

ENTERPRISE TODAY

Enterprise rode its focus on the home market segment from humble beginnings all the way to passing Hertz in 1996 (according to Funding Universe) as the number 1 player in the *entire* rental car industry in the United States. And it appears to be adding to its lead.

In fact, the company had reached a strong enough position as of 1995 to announce that it would now compete for the business of the travel segment. This raises the question: Is this an inevitable move of a company that needs to find growth, or the first step in its eventual decline? So far it seems to be working out for Enterprise, but one thing seems clear: the focus on the home market segment fueled an incredible run from nowhere to number 1 in a massive industry and illuminated some brilliant strategies that probably would not have been possible with divided corporate attention and resources.

DUPLICATING ENTERPRISE'S STRATEGY IN YOUR INDUSTRY

SEGMENT ATTRACTIVENESS

Enterprise instilled its focus through its management team's instincts, led by Jack Taylor. Encouraged by the impact of some brilliant strategies that we've just outlined, the company was able to stay the course long enough to become the dominant player in its industry.

How can you develop the type of winning focus that Enterprise demonstrates? To help answer that question, we have built a framework called Segment Attractiveness. The tool creates an explicit formula that companies can use to intelligently—and consistently—evaluate its choices and make smart targeting decisions.

The tool is best used to help allocate focus from among several potential customer segments. However, we've also learned that companies can use this tool in a wide variety of situations—to determine the attractiveness of different market segments, potential acquisitions, and specific customer deals. Mary even used it to evaluate different options when buying a new home.

Used most effectively, the Segment Attractiveness tool builds on the needs-based segmentation work we described in the previous chapter to drive customer segment focus. In addition, you can turbo-charge the effectiveness of the tool by using it in conjunction with the Ability to Compete and Prioritizer tools that we will describe in the next two chapters.

BUILDING THE LIGHT VERSION OF THE SEGMENT ATTRACTIVENESS ANALYSIS, STEP-BY-STEP: WHO DO YOU LOVE?

Step 1: The first step in completing a Segment Attractiveness analysis is to complete a statement that starts out like this:

"At (our company), we **love** segments (or markets or deals) that . . ."

Complete this statement by brainstorming 10 to 15 *criteria of attractiveness.* These are characteristics that allow you to answer the question: If you could build the perfect segment (or market), what would the attitudes, behaviors, and or needs of its customers be? What would the segment's *characteristics* be? For example, "We love segments that like to partner to develop a new solution" or "We love segments that are growing." The light Segment Attractiveness example that follows for the Enterprise case you just read illustrates some sample criteria.

Step 2: The next step is to whittle down the brainstormed criteria of attractiveness list to five or six of the most important ones; having too many will complicate the exercise.

In a light version of the Segment Attractiveness framework, such as our example in Figure 5.3, you would then use these criteria to rate which of your potential targets most embody these characteristics.

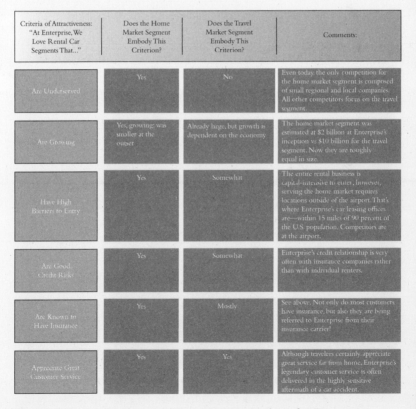

Criteria of Attractiveness: "At Enterprise, We Love Rental Car Segments That..."	Does the Home Market Segment Embody This Criterion?	Does the Travel Market Segment Embody This Criterion?	Comments:
Are Underserved	Yes	No	Even today, the only competition for the home market segment is composed of small regional and local companies. All other competitors focus on the travel segment.
Are Growing	Yes, growing; was smaller at the outset	Already large, but growth is dependent on the economy	The home market segment was estimated at $2 billion at Enterprise's inception vs $10 billion for the travel segment. Now they are roughly equal in size.
Have High Barriers to Entry	Yes	Somewhat	The entire rental business is capital-intensive to enter; however, serving the home market requires locations outside of the airport. That's where Enterprise's car leasing offices are—within 15 miles of 90 percent of the U.S. population. Competitors are at the airport.
Are Good Credit Risks	Yes	Somewhat	Enterprise's credit relationship is very often with insurance companies rather than with individual renters.
Are Known to Have Insurance	Yes	Mostly	See above. Not only do most customers have insurance, but also they are being referred to Enterprise from their insurance carrier!
Appreciate Great Customer Service	Yes	Yes	Although travelers certainly appreciate great service far from home, Enterprise's legendary customer service is often delivered in the highly sensitive aftermath of a car accident.

Figure 5.3   Light Segment Attractiveness Analysis for Enterprise

(*continued*)

(*continued*)

Enterprise must have faced constant pressure to dilute its focus and also target the travel segment. We believe that even a light analysis like the one in Figure 5.3 would have removed any temptation. However, if you like a little more precision, the full version of the Segment Attractiveness exercise is for you.

THE FULL VERSION OF THE SEGMENT ATTRACTIVENESS ANALYSIS IS MORE QUANTITATIVE

Step 3: The full version follows the same process as the light, but adds two more quantitative elements. First, you weight the five or six final attractiveness criteria according to their importance to a company.

Step 4: Next, each potential segment is rated on a scale of 1 to 10 (rather than a yes/no/somewhat scale as illustrated in the light version) to indicate how well each segment embodies each criterion. The product of the weight and rate enable a specific, comparable attractiveness score for each segment. Within the case that follows, we have illustrated a full version of the analysis. You can skip right to it or review the accompanying interesting case to further your understanding of the power of Segment Attractiveness.

THINK OF SEGMENT ATTRACTIVENESS AS A SHIELD THAT NOT ONLY PROTECTS FOCUS BUT CAN ALSO CLARIFY IT

This case was brought to us by longtime consultant, colleague, and friend Tom Niehaus. A new drug to treat acquired immunodeficiency syndrome (AIDS) was struggling when it was introduced in the 1990s—and the drug's marketers couldn't figure out why.

At the time, an AIDS diagnosis was considered an almost certain death sentence. The drug was a potential cure and the stock market was expecting a blockbuster, so its relative lack of success was concerning and somewhat baffling.

There *was* a drawback that the company's strategists had to acknowledge: the drug had potentially harmful side effects that were similar to the consequences of chemotherapy.

In addition, the sales force had reported back to the marketers that a certain percentage of doctors had been extremely fascinated by the drug's chemistry and method of action. This seemed anecdotal to the marketers, but they took note of the feedback nonetheless.

The strategic moves that led to the drug's eventual success illustrate the power of combining last chapter's subject, Segmentation, with the concept featured in this chapter, Segment Attractiveness.

Segmentation

Previously, this AIDS drug had been marketed in the same way to all the doctors in the company's markets. Marketers realized that the drug's plusses and minuses would appeal—or not appeal—to doctors with different needs. They used a segmentation process similar to the one described in the last chapter and segmented doctors into six distinct groups as defined in the following section.

One dimension considered doctors in terms of *how aggressively* they treated patients. Some were more open to trying new approaches in the hope of curing a patient, whereas others took a more cautious approach. Information available via the IMS Health database allowed the company to clearly see where individual doctors fit on this scale.

The second dimension revealed a doctor's *primary professional focus.* Certainly all doctors care about patients, but some were especially devoted to patient care to the exclusion of most business matters and with only a passing interest in science. Others, although devoted to patients, were more business-like in their orientation and were segmented as Money Makers. A third group had a higher-than-average interest in the research and science aspects of being a doctor (Scientists). The company's sales reps knew doctors well enough to know where each fit on this dimension.

Putting the two dimensions together created six doctor segments, as shown in Figure 5.4.

(continued)

(continued)

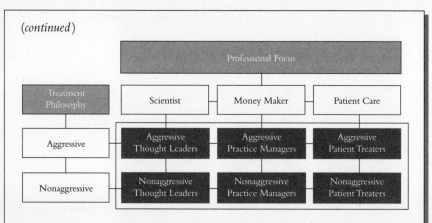

Figure 5.4 Two Key Dimensions: Professional Focus and Treatment Philosophy

Segment Attractiveness

After completing the segmentation analysis, the company followed up with a segment attractiveness exercise. In brainstorming what the perfect doctor segment's attitudes, needs, behaviors, and characteristics would be, they first settled on the practical reality that the targeted segments had to be at least *large and growing enough* to support company revenue goals. They also had to be reasonably accessible and easy to reach with the company's marketing messages. (See the first three Criteria of Attractiveness in the Full Segment Attractive Analysis shown in Figure 5.5.)

Then the team moved on to the segments' ideal characteristics as they related to *this particular drug.* The product's unique attributes meant that they were looking for segments that would be either fascinated by the drug's interesting chemistry or willing to take on the risks of the drug's possibly harmful side effects in order to try to find a cure for the potentially fatal disease.

Using the full version of the tool, the company created a Criteria of Attractiveness, weighted the criteria, and rated each segment. See the column headers for each segment and how each segment rated on each Criteria of Attractiveness. Then the team multiplied each rating by the Criteria of Attractiveness weighting to create a total attractiveness score for each segment.

Segments

"We like segments or markets that…": Criteria of Attractiveness	Weighting (1-100)	Aggressive Thought Leaders		Nonaggressive Thought Leaders		Aggressive Practice Managers		Nonaggressive Practice Managers		Aggressive Patient Treaters		Nonaggressive Patient Treaters	
		Rating (1-10)	Score	Rating (1-10)	Score	Rating (1-10)	Score	Rating (1-10)	Score	Rating (1-10)	Score	Rating (1-10)	Score
Are Large	20	3	60	3	60	6	120	6	120	7	140	8	160
Are Growing in Size	10	3	30	3	30	6	60	8	80	5	50	5	50
Are Easy to Reach	10	8	80	7	70	8	80	7	70	5	50	4	40
Are Scientific and Interested in Novel Chemistry	20	9	180	8	160	3	60	2	40	5	100	4	80
Are Willing to Try New Things	20	7	140	4	80	6	120	4	80	8	160	2	40
Less Concerned about Potential Lawsuits	20	4	80	2	40	1	20	1	20	7	140	2	40
	100	Total:	570	Total:	440	Total:	460	Total:	410	Total:	640	Total:	410

Figure 5.5 Full Segment Attractiveness Analysis: Which Segment Is the Most Attractive?

(*continued*)

Based on the total scores, the company decided to target just two of the six segments for a while. The lower ratings for certain segments showed that the prospectively harsh side effects would scare off any doctors with nonaggressive treatment philosophies until there was further proof for the drug's efficacy.

They also eliminated the Aggressive Practice Managers segment because of its lower attractiveness scores. These doctors were so worried about their bottom lines that they would likely avoid the drug until further experience was gained out of fear for potential lawsuits.

On the bright side, the Aggressive Patient Treaters segment seemed like a logical target because its higher attractiveness score. Positioning the AIDS drug as a potential lifesaver would appeal to these doctors willing to take any risk to try to save a dying patient. But was one target segment out of six enough to meet aggressive growth targets for the drug?

That was when the marketers remembered the anecdotal feedback from the sales force about the product's interesting chemistry. By touting an "innovative new approach to treating AIDS" to the Aggressive Thought Leaders segment, the company found a group of leading edge thinkers who could serve as a potential proving ground for the treatment.

The company promoted to Aggressive Patient Treaters through face-to-face visits via the sales force, and to the Aggressive Thought Leaders through academic conferences.

By looking at the adoption data of the drug (Figure 5.6), see if you can guess the timing of the academic conferences. Although the Aggressive Thought Leaders were only about 10 percent of total doctors, they clearly influenced all of the other segments.

Through targeting two segments with the appropriate messages, the drug caught a fresh restart, and based on the successes and word of mouth from the target segments, the rest of the segments followed! (Note: In Figure 5.6, the legend refers to the six segments described above.)

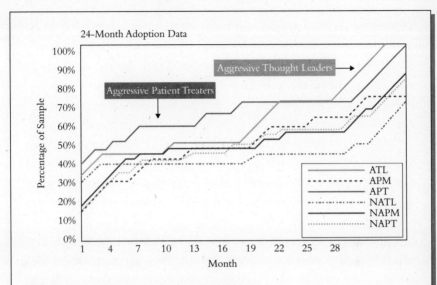

Figure 5.6   New Drug Adoption Curve

There are many lessons to be learned from this and the Enterprise story, but most relevant to the subject of this chapter is the following: *just because you have discovered several segments in your market doesn't mean you target all of them.* By choosing targets that are a particularly good fit for your company or product's capabilities, you not only operate more efficiently but tend to grow larger in those segments and even draw in business from other segments.

TIPS FOR BUILDING EFFECTIVE SEGMENT ATTRACTIVENESS ANALYSES

Clients often ask us, "How do we know if we have this analysis right?" The answer lies in *ensuring alignment* at two key junctures of this analysis.

First, it is crucial to get as much agreement as possible from your executive management team regarding the criteria of attractiveness formula. These criteria should reflect their reality—meaning it would be how they currently make decisions . . . or how they would plan to make decisions in the future. The more people who share the definition of what an attractive segment, opportunity, or deal looks like, the better.

(continued)

(*continued*)

Second, *each segment's rating* ought to come from as broad a group of internal and external experts as possible. Many spirited debates will ensue in all parts of this analysis, but once alignment on the criteria and ratings is won, businesses gain new clarity about which markets, customers, and even partners must be pursued—or, just as importantly, ignored.

Of course, using this tool to determine segment attractiveness requires that *you segment your market to begin with*. So it's essential to understand and apply Chapter 3's content. And as you will see, you can add some other pieces of analysis to Segment Attractiveness to make it even more powerful.

In the next chapter, we'll show you an additional framework that will help with targeting, creating differentiation, value propositions, and much more. Get ready for the Ability to Compete tool, the most versatile tool in the kit!

CHAPTER 6

What *Were* They Smoking?

How Using an Ability to Win Analysis Could Have Saved Volkswagen Millions

POWER TOOL: ABILITY TO WIN

He who knows others is wise; he who knows himself is enlightened.

—Lao Tzu, philosopher of ancient China, best known
as the author of the *Tao Te Ching*

A TALE OF TWO CAR COMPANIES

The picture of the Volkswagen (VW) Phaeton (Figure 6.1) is just like the one featured in an infamous advertisement for the car headlined "What Were You Guys Smoking?" We were unable to obtain the permission to reprint the ad in this book, perhaps for reasons that will become clear as you read this chapter. The headline and body copy of the piece suggest that the Phaeton design team must have been "in a good place" when they conceived of the car.

Unfortunately, the ad introduced one the most disappointing North American automobile sales performances since Ford's Edsel debacle in the late 1950s. The VW Phaeton was designed to compete with luxury class automobiles like the Mercedes-Benz S-Class.

Figure 6.1   Picture of a Volkswagen Phaeton

In the coming pages, you'll understand why Phaeton's flawed marketing strategy was a big reason for its failure in the largest automobile market in the world. You will also see how Toyota's Lexus brand conquered the exact same challenge on the road to its phenomenal success.

Most important, these two cases will provide a proper introduction to the most powerful tool we can show you, something we call the Ability to Win. The tool leverages three critical pieces of information:

- A deep understanding of *customer needs*
- Knowledge of your own *company's capabilities*
- Awareness of *customers' perceptions* about you and your competitors

By combining these three elements into one analysis, Ability to Win shows companies exactly why they are—or are not—succeeding. Even more important, the framework draws out which strategies will and won't work in differentiating products and brands from those of competitors.

The Ability to Win tool trumps the overused and misguided SWOT analysis that many of our companies use in their brand plans. As many are likely aware, a SWOT is a one-page summary of a brand's strengths, weaknesses, opportunities, and threats. We are very anti-SWOT because the analysis ignores customer needs and perceptions. After all, what good is a strength if it doesn't deliver something *customers desire?*

When a company believes it's bringing a particular strength or advantage to the market that actually turns out to be something customers *don't care about,* they get into trouble. Worse, when customers view an internally perceived strength as a weakness, it can cost millions of dollars. That is what happened in the case of the Volkswagen Phaeton—and it cost *hundreds* of millions.

The Ability to Win framework should be used before building a SWOT analysis, because it is customer-focused. Our tool leads companies to examine their capabilities and perceptions by focusing on customer needs instead of ignoring them. It also forces companies to face some hard but essential facts about themselves; often, they come to see that they're not in as strong of a position in the market as they initially thought. Fortunately, they achieve this self-awareness *before* they invest—and therefore waste—millions on value propositions that customers ignore.

Ability to Win analysis is a wake-up call that ultimately directs strategy toward what really matters to target customers. We believe it is our most valuable tool—and we hope you also gain an appreciation for it as you read the following chapter.

A COMPETITOR'S AGGRESSIVE MOVE MAY HAVE SPARKED THE PHAETON CONCEPT

Most successful people are extremely competitive by nature—and many executives' careers have been fueled by a desire to continuously pummel competitors and dominate markets.

But uber-competitors can often become *so* focused on their rivals that they forget about their customers. Focusing solely on one-upping a rival's features and functions is a recipe for disaster.

Perhaps competitive drive is the reason why the VW organization became obsessed with the notion of a VW luxury car in the early 2000s. Upscale automaker Mercedes-Benz had recently stepped on VW's toes by introducing a lower-cost A-Class model. VW likely perceived the car to be a direct competitor in the mid-market.

But rather than protect VW's strong position in mid- and lower-priced segments and stay focused—à la Southwest and Enterprise—VW wanted to continue the fight. The idea was to counter Mercedes-Benz' step-down with a stepped-up Volkswagen brand.

Curiously, VW already had a division, Audi, that competed in the luxury car market. But the Audi A8 was positioned as a "sporty" brand within the full-size luxury sedan market. VW wanted this new brand, dubbed the Volkswagen Phaeton, to be more of a comfort-oriented, limousine-like car that would compare with the likes of the Mercedes-Benz S-Class. The VW team thought that the VW brand—given its heritage and favorable image in the automotive market—would be a key strength of the offering.

VW chairman Ferdinand Piech charged a team of VW engineers with building a car that had 10 lofty feature-and-function parameters. One parameter was that the car should be able to be driven all day at 185 mph in 120-degree heat while maintaining an internal temperature of 72 degrees. The other nine were also very ambitious.

It's not clear where these parameters came from, but given their extreme specifications, it's a good bet that they didn't come from significant consumer research. It *is* clear that the VW team wanted their Phaeton to surpass the design engineering standards set by Mercedes-Benz and BMW.

VW's competitiveness may have obscured the fact that Mercedes-Benz and BMW had been making high-end vehicles for decades. They have substantial reputations and knowledge of the luxury market.

But this was a big organizational project—and perhaps because of that, no one had the courage to ask the obvious questions: Did the VW engineers, skilled at building great mainstream automobiles, have the capabilities to deliver on the Phaeton vision? Did the Phaeton team have a deep enough understanding of the needs of the luxury car buyer to guide their design and marketing decisions?

LEXUS WAS ALSO SPARKED BY A CHAIRMAN'S CHALLENGE—BUT THE SIMILARITIES END THERE

Ironically, a similar situation had emerged roughly 20 years earlier during a 1983 meeting at the Japan-based auto manufacturer Toyota. Then-chairman

Eiji Toyoda tasked his company executives with the question: "Can we create a luxury vehicle to challenge the world's best?"

Like VW, competitive pressures may have also been driving Toyota's entrée into luxury cars. Fellow Japanese automakers Honda and Nissan had both recently announced plans to produce upscale cars.

But the Toyota project, which led to the creation of the Lexus brand, proceeded very differently. While the VW Phaeton engineers focused internally and began working on building a car that embodied 10 predefined (and probably internally defined) parameters, Toyota focused *externally* on the market—a market the Japanese company realized they needed to know much more about.

A SURPRISING STRATEGY FOR LEXUS IN ITS HOME MARKET OF JAPAN

One of the Toyota's first decisions was to *exclude* Japan—Toyota's home market—in the Lexus launch. At the time, Toyota already sold two larger sedans, the Century and the Crown, only in Japan. There were some significant insights behind this decision:

- Introducing Lexus in Japan could create considerable brand confusion. The typical Japanese luxury car buyer might think the Lexus was just a dressed-up Toyota Century or Crown with a higher price.
- Japanese luxury trends were being driven more and more by Western world tastes. They believed that establishing the Lexus brand outside of Japan first, particularly in the United States, might eventually clear up any potential brand confusion and create demand for Lexus in Japan later.

It couldn't have been an easy decision to exclude its home market in this venture, but these insights appear to have worked out very well for Toyota. Lexus's initial focus on the U.S. market was a huge success, followed by an entrance into the European market, which finally drove demand for the cars in Japan. But the company showed remarkable restraint and patience in ensuring the potential brand confusion in Japan was cleared up before introducing Lexus at home in 2005, *16 years* after the product's 1989 launch!

PHAETON ENGINEERS CONTINUE TENDING TO "THE LIST"; LEXUS IMMERSES ITS TEAM IN THE MARKET

Unlike Lexus, VW did *not* exclude its home market of Germany in the Phaeton's launch plans, which turned out to be a good decision—because Germany is one of the few markets where the brand has any significant sales today.

It was clear that the U.S. market, with its affluent consumers and industry-leading luxury car sales, would be critical to success for both Lexus and Phaeton brands. Once again, the different ways that each company reacted to this common fact is instructive.

Toyota sent Lexus team members to rent a home in Laguna Beach, California. Their mission: understand the lifestyles and tastes of the American luxury consumer so they could get the value proposition right in a segment that was new for the company.

It appears that the Phaeton team continued to largely focus on the original list of 10 features. The resulting lack of understanding of U.S. luxury car buyers would, by most accounts, contribute significantly to the downfall of the VW Phaeton: the insights that Toyota and Lexus gained in California would act as the catalyst of their success.

PHAETON ENGINEERS DELIVER AN INTERESTING CAR, BUT IS IT IN "GOOD TASTE"?

Armed with their checklist, the Phaeton design engineers *did* create a very interesting car. Indeed, more than 100 patents tied specifically to the brand are registered.

Designing products for an upscale market when you are used to mainstream tastes is tricky, though. It's easy to overdo it.

The 2004 prelaunch previews of the Phaeton met with mixed reviews. There was praise for a lot of its design features, such as the four-zone climate control system, air compressor suspension, and other features inspired by Piech's original list.

However, most reviewers agreed that that the number of the car's features—contributing to a $70,000+ price tag—were over the top. In its zeal to out-engineer BMW and Mercedes-Benz, the Phaeton had been over-engineered.

Making matters worse, it may have been under-engineered in one area considered very important to luxury car buyers: *performance*. Specifically, designers had decided to use an all-steel platform for the Phaeton, rather than leverage the aluminum platform of its sister brand, Audi.

Many believed that the car was too heavy, which diminished the Phaeton's acceleration and fuel economy performance. A 12-cylinder option (in addition to a standard 8-cylinder version) may have been a performance-enhancing necessity. It added some zip but further reduced the car's fuel economy.

Perhaps if the brand had been guided by customer insight rather than the list, the brand would have gotten the balance right. By failing to seek more market research, VW probably put too much pressure on its design engineers. Ultimately, it appears that the company overestimated its luxury car engineering capabilities by expecting to get the design right based primarily on a list of preconceived features.

LEXUS ENGINEERS GET IT MOSTLY RIGHT

Many of the Lexus engineers were used to designing Toyotas and were moving up-market in their design project as well. The difference? The company understood that the only way to improve the engineer's design skills was to learn what luxury car buyers really wanted. They were interested in meeting these customers' needs, not just bludgeoning aggressive competitors.

The team's immersion into Laguna Beach's affluent culture drove many aspects of the successful Lexus value proposition. From a design standpoint, the introduction of the LS 400 was hailed by experts for the automobile's quietness, well-appointed and ergonomic interior, engine performance, build quality, aerodynamics, fuel economy, and value. Still, like the Phaeton, there were some performance-related criticisms.

However, Lexus's efforts to understand its market enabled the team to create the perception of a fine luxury automobile. Its initial campaign, called "The Relentless Pursuit of Perfection," showed a pyramid of champagne glasses on

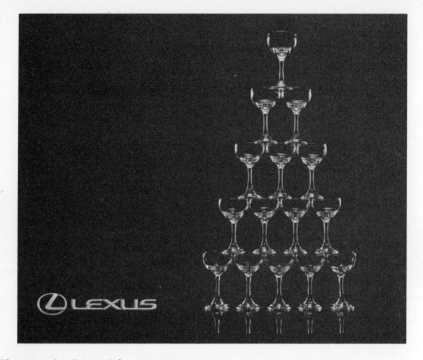

Figure 6.2   Lexus Advertisement

the hood of a Lexus undisturbed by the car's purring engine. The image was powerful enough that Lexus excluded the actual car in later print ads and still got the message across (Figure 6.2).

Compare this to the somewhat unusual Phaeton "What Were You Guys Smoking" headline mentioned at the beginning of this chapter and ask yourself the following question: Which brand seemed like the tasteful newcomer to the luxury car market, and which seemed like the clunky party crasher at the debutante ball?

PERCEPTION IS REALITY

The vast differences in the two brand's approaches to understanding customer needs and evaluating their own capabilities should be clear by now. But Lexus's desire and ability to understand luxury car buyer *perceptions*— compared with Phaeton's *misperceptions*—were an even bigger factor in each brand's fortunes.

Lexus' study revealed a top priority of luxury car buyers in the U.S. market: status. Above all, U.S. buyers wanted their expensive car to be a *symbol of their success*. And because Toyota was synonymous with more mainstream vehicles, using the parent company's brand on the Lexus would *not* deliver the sense of "having arrived" to buyers. The company therefore decided to use the Lexus brand on the car exclusively. In fact, no mention of the Toyota brand would be made in marketing Lexus.

This was an expensive decision because it involved more than just a brand name and symbol. The U.S. luxury car buyer also expected a well-rounded ownership experience, including a classy car-buying process and highly attentive service after the sale. So separation from the Toyota brand required a completely new dealership and service infrastructure for Lexus, separate and apart from Toyota's existing U.S. retail sites.

LEXUS PROVES IT "GETS IT" DURING A RECALL

Rather than resist the investment, Lexus embraced the challenge of establishing a world-class dealership and service network. Famously, they partnered with Ritz-Carlton to train retail and service personnel on the white-glove ways of the world's most exclusive hotel.

With its plan and infrastructure in place, Lexus launched in the United States in September 1989—and faced a significant challenge almost immediately.

In November 1989, Lexus conducted a recall of all 8,000 vehicles it had sold to date, reportedly based on two customer complaints about defective wiring and an overheated brake light. To have this occur so close to the brand launch, it seemed like the timing for the recall couldn't have been worse.

Making matters more difficult was the fact that VW's Audi had recently conducted a recall in the United States to correct "unintended acceleration." There were reports that the cars would start accelerating even though the driver did not have a foot on the gas pedal.

Although the claims ultimately proved to be unsubstantiated, Audi had handled the recall very slowly and defensively. It was a public relations disaster from which the brand did not recover for more than a decade—and the entire incident made any automobile recall operation extremely risky.

It is often said that how one handles difficult times determines a brand's ultimate success or failure. Because they were able to draw upon their knowledge of affluent customer service needs, Lexus passed their recall test with flying colors.

In stark contrast to Audi's plodding ways, Lexus resolved the reported issues on every one of the 8,000 vehicles it had sold in just 20 days. It sent technicians to pick up, repair, and return cars to customers in just a few days, free of charge. In addition, it flew in technicians and rented garage space to fix the issue for owners in remote locations.

Industry watchers lauded the way that Lexus handled the recall. The resulting positive word of mouth from owners helped establish the brand as one that delivers status through a true luxury ownership experience. Sales results exploded upward the following year.

"LEAVE YOUR BMW AT HOME; WE'LL TAKE MY LEXUS. . ."

Today, Lexus continues to find ways to meet the status-seeking needs of its affluent target market. Figure 6.3 is an excerpt from a recent Lexus promotional program.

The map in the figure shows a Lexus lot as the closest parking for fans attending events at Atlanta's Turner Field baseball stadium several years ago. At the time, parking at Atlanta Braves' games for Lexus owners was free.[1]

Imagine the joy—and boost to his personal sense of status—that a Lexus owner feels when telling his BMW or Mercedes-Benz-owning friends that he will drive to the game. Why? Because he can park *right beside the stadium* for free. And imagine all of the non-Lexus-owning status seekers walking by this well-positioned parking lot, consciously or unconsciously adding Lexus to the short list of vehicles they will consider the next time they are in the market!

---

[1] The Lexus lot concept at Atlanta's Turner Field has been replaced with a slightly broader concept called The Nalley Lot, featuring free parking for owners of vehicles from the Nalley dealerships. The Nalley dealerships encompass a number of luxury brands, including Lexus.

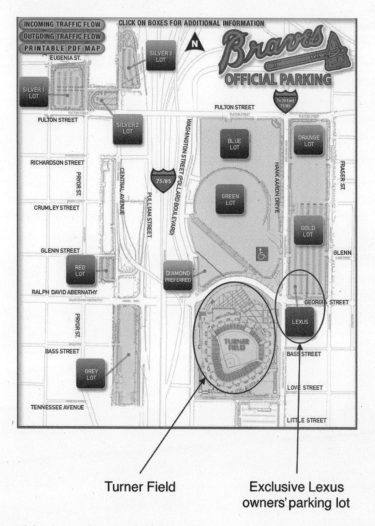

Figure 6.3 Lexus Promotional Program

"THE PEOPLE'S CAR" AS A LUXURY BRAND?

In stark contrast to Lexus/Toyota, Phaeton/VW made the decision to *not* separate Phaeton dealership and service centers from its existing U.S. retail sites selling other VW passenger cars. In fact, Phaeton fully embraced the VW brand and infrastructure in its marketing.

This is evident from the "What Were You Guys Smoking" advertisement mentioned previously. The ad shows the Phaeton positioned similarly to the photo at the start of the chapter—with the VW badge prominently displayed on the back of the Phaeton. VW made the mistake of thinking the brand's name, which translated into English means "the people's car," was an asset.

But in customers' minds, the VW badge was a *detriment* to a luxury car brand. Who wants to buy the people's car when they feel like they have finally risen above the masses and made it in the world? The result was a disastrous performance, especially as compared with the first two years of the Lexus introduction (Figure 6.4).

By 1991, three years after its introduction, Lexus was already racking up huge sales and stealing customers from American-made luxury brands like Lincoln and Cadillac. The brand's strength has continued to this day; it was the number 1 premium-selling car in the United States *every year* for the entire decade of 2000–2010.

Contrast this with Phaeton's results through its first three years. After selling 820 cars in the United States in 2005, the company had stopped selling the car completely in the North American market.

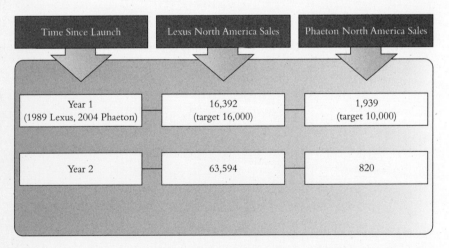

Figure 6.4   Relative Performance of Lexus's First Two Years' Sales (1989–1990) to Phaeton's First Two Years' Sales (2004–2005)

Source: Lexus figures from Chester Dawson's *Lexus: The Relentless Pursuit*; the Phaeton's 2004 sales were from an article at www.autonews.com; and the Phaeton's 2005 sales were from an article at www.motortrend.com.

The Phaeton brand does continue to exist today, with a majority of its sales coming from its home market of Germany. VW's state-of-the-art factory, designed to churn out multitudes of Phaetons, has been operating at a fraction of its capacity.

Rumors of a Phaeton introduction into the Chinese market and/or a reintroduction in the United States abound. According to *Motor Trend,* the model will be positioned as a luxury car for people who don't want to show off.

No estimates have been published about how much the failed brand has cost VW, but it must be in the hundreds of millions.

CUSTOMER PERCEPTION IS REALITY

Here is one of the many lessons to be learned from this remarkable tale: if a company *thinks it is good* at delivering on a benefit sought or value and the customer has the opposite perception, it's the customer's perception that counts.

INTRODUCING THE POWER TOOL: ABILITY TO WIN

THE TOOL THAT COULD HAVE SAVED VOLKSWAGEN MILLIONS

The logical question is, how can a company get it right like Lexus and avoid the mistakes of the Phaeton in *any* market—not just automobiles? In our opinion, the Ability to Win is the best analysis tool to allow you to properly assess the three critical pieces of information that made the difference between Lexus success and Phaeton's failure—which again, are:

- A deep understanding of *customer needs*
- Knowledge of your own *company's capabilities*
- Awareness of *customers perceptions* about you and your competitors

(*continued*)

(continued)

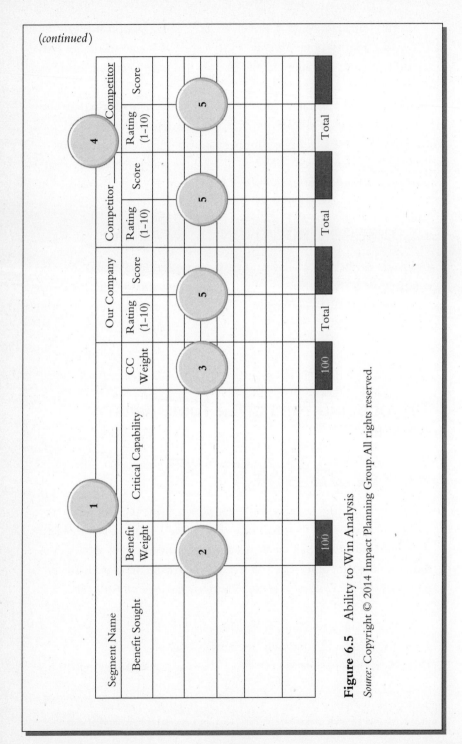

Figure 6.5 Ability to Win Analysis

We'll introduce the workings of the Ability to Win tool here, and then show in the remaining chapters how you can leverage the analysis to create a winning approach, message, and offer.

The tool, shown in Figure 6.5, looks intimidating at first. But, through illustrating its use in the context of the Lexus/Phaeton case study, you'll learn that it's quite user-friendly.

We will compare the two brands and one additional competitor, BMW, in creating a fictitious Ability to Win analysis. Each step in the process of completing the analysis is signified by a numbered dot in Figure 6.5 and will be fully described.

STEPS 1 AND 2: IDENTIFYING THE TARGET SEGMENT AND WHAT THEY WANT

As Lexus demonstrated, understanding your target segment and their needs is crucial. Most of the information from steps 1 and 2 in the Ability to Win tool can be brought over from your previous efforts in identifying benefits sought and customer values (see Chapter 2), defining segments (see Chapter 3), and determining segment attractiveness (see Chapter 5).

However, one important additional task is necessary to complete step 2 of the Ability to Win tool: figuring out the weight or relative importance of each customer benefit sought or value. Specifically, if a customer could spread 100 points across all of the benefits sought, how many points would they give to each?

Let's consider this chapter's case. What if we were to query luxury car buyers in the United States about the benefits sought and customer values that were important to them and to weight them according to importance? We might see a partially filled-out Ability to Win tool as shown in Figure 6.6.

(continued)

(*continued*)

Segment: North American Luxury Car Buyers				Our Company		Competitor 1		Competitor 2	
Benefit Sought	Benefit Weight	Critical Capability	CC Weight	Rating (1-10)	Score	Rating (1-10)	Score	Rating (1-10)	Score
Status	50								
Performance & Style	25								
Ownership Experience	25								
	100		100	Total		Total		Total	

Figure 6.6 Ability to Win: Steps 1 and 2

We can see here that status (with 50 points) is the most important benefit sought to the segment, followed by equal weightings for performance and style and ownership experience.

Note that you *can* utilize all five benefits sought spaces in the template (most of our clients do). But in Chapter 3 we discussed using the Occam's razor approach to simplify segmentation. The same mind-set can apply here as well, where three benefits have explained the most important benefits sought by the customer. On to the next step . . .

STEP 3: IDENTIFYING THE CRITICAL CAPABILITIES NEEDED TO DELIVER ON THE BENEFIT SOUGHT

Critical capabilities are the assets and skills that *any* company needs to deliver on a benefit sought (not just your company). The Ability to Win analysis requires a company to identify the two most important critical capabilities to accompany each benefit sought. It also calls for a further spreading of the benefit weight across the critical capabilities.

Marketers must ask the following two questions about each benefit sought to generate a list of critical capabilities:

1. "If we were starting a company, what would be the two most important assets or skills we'd need to deliver on this benefit?"

   Note that you will probably come up with more than two critical capabilities. Pick the most important two, *not* the two that you are best at! For instance, if a customer benefit sought is customer support, you may have the best warranty program; however, it may not be the most critical thing that could contribute to a customer's benefit. Instead, 24-hour hotline support may be more important.

2. "Given that benefit X has a weighting of Y, how would a customer spread those points across the critical capabilities according to *their* importance?"

Segment: North American Luxury Car Buyers				Our Company		Competitor___		Competitor___	
Benefit Sought	Benefit Weight	Critical Capability	CC Weight	Rating (1-10)	Score	Rating (1-10)	Score	Rating (1-10)	Score
Status	50	Brand Image	40						
		Ownership Perks	10						
Performance & Style	25	Design Engineering	15						
		Amenities	10						
Ownership Experience	25	Classy Dealerships	15						
		World-Class Service	10						
	100		100	Total		Total		Total	

Figure 6.7   Ability to Win: Step 3

Source: Copyright © 2014 Impact Planning Group. All rights reserved.

(continued)

(continued)

Further building out our chapter example, the Ability to Win analysis might look like Figure 6.7 after step 3 is completed.

To further illustrate this example, brand image and ownership perks are considered the two most important critical capabilities to deliver on the benefit sought of status. And you can see that of these two critical capabilities, brand image—receiving a score of 40—is much more important to customers than the ownership perks (which only got a 10).

STEP 4: IDENTIFYING THE COMPETITORS TO RATE YOUR ABILITY TO WIN AGAINST

This step is not as easy as it sounds. Most companies will choose to complete the tool using two or three competitors at the most. But because you probably have more than two or three important competitors, it's critical to choose whom you will bring into the analysis wisely.

The best advice is to choose the competitors that your segment considers *their most viable alternatives.* If you completed the work from Chapter 4, you will have a good list to choose from.

Where this choice can get tricky is when one of your customers' best competitive alternatives is an *indirect* competitor of your company. We have worked with several companies whose products help people stop smoking. Our clients in this space always have to consider the cold turkey competitive option that consumers have. This refers to quitting smoking without any pharmaceutical medicines or over-the-counter products at all.

The brand teams always gain some important learning about the advantages *and* disadvantages of using their solution to stop smoking compared to doing it on their own. Similarly, in many business-to-business service markets we find that clients can often choose to do nothing or do it themselves instead of pay our client to provide services for them. In new markets, these self-reliant options are often the *only* competitor of an innovative product or service.

In our example in Figure 6.8, we model three direct competitors in the North American luxury car buying segment. We will put Lexus into

Segment: North American Luxury Car Buyers				Lexus		VW Phaeton		BMW	
Benefit Sought	Benefit Weight	Critical Capability	CC Weight	Rating (1-10)	Score	Rating (1-10)	Score	Rating (1-10)	Score
Status	50	Brand Image	40						
		Ownership Perks	10						
Performance & Style	25	Design Engineering	15						
		Amenities	10						
Ownership Experience	25	Classy Dealerships	15						
		World-Class Service	10						
	100		100	Total		Total		Total	

Figure 6.8 Ability to Win: Step 4

the spot for "Our Company" and model Lexus's ability to win versus VW's Phaeton and BMW.

STEP 5: RATING ALL COMPANIES ON THE CRITICAL CAPABILITIES—*FROM THE CUSTOMER'S PERSPECTIVE*

The final step in the Ability to Win process (before analyzing results) is to rate your company and your competitors on how well you *currently* deliver on each critical capability. *However, you must rate each company— including yours—from the* customer's perspective, *not your own.*

This is a crucial point. If you give yourself high ratings, you may likely be deluding yourself. Do you think that the Phaeton team, using the VW brand, would have rated *themselves* high or low on the critical capability of brand image? Clearly, they thought that the VW badge was strength in delivering the status that luxury car buyers seek. But in reality, how did luxury car buyers—their target customers—view VW's brand image as a

(continued)

(continued)

status symbol in reality? And whose perception really mattered: VW's or their customers'?

As has been said many times in the past, perception is reality. And in marketing, it's the customer's perception that counts.

Using a scale of 1 to 10 (no zeros allowed) to rate each company on each critical capability *from the customer's perspective,* Figure 6.9 shows how luxury buyers might have scored our two case study competitors and BMW in our sample Ability to Win.

Segment: North American Luxury Car Buyers				Lexus		VW Phaeton		BMW	
Benefit Sought	Benefit Weight	Critical Capability	CC Weight	Rating (1-10)	Score	Rating (1-10)	Score	Rating (1-10)	Score
Status	50	Brand Image	40	8	320	2	80	9	360
		Ownership Perks	10	9	90	2	20	7	70
Performance & Style	25	Design Engineering	15	6	90	5	75	9	135
		Amenities	10	6	60	9	90	8	80
Ownership Experience	25	Classy Dealerships	15	8	120	2	30	8	120
		World-Class Service	10	9	90	5	50	7	70
	100		100	Total	770	Total	345	Total	835

Figure 6.9 Ability to Win: Completed

Source: Copyright © 2014 Impact Planning Group. All rights reserved.

The Ability to Win total scores are a proxy for how much value customers believe each competitor is bringing to the marketplace.

ABILITY TO WIN ANALYSIS

Although this analysis is fictitious, it goes a long way to explain what happened in the case. Phaeton's amenities, which drove 100 patents and mostly met VW's lofty goals for the brand, were likely superior even to those of the engineering "machine" that is BMW (as indicated by Phaeton's high ratings for amenities in the analysis), but this was only one of several critical capabilities that mattered to the luxury car buyer.

VW's decisions to use the VW badge on the car, to not invest in separate dealerships, and to over-engineer the car were fatal to its efforts in the massive U.S. car market. The low scores in these highly weighted areas of importance to the customers could have been a red flag to VW that the Phaeton project was in trouble.

Perhaps the fate of both companies was sealed by the first move each made after they launched a luxury car manufacturing initiative. VW immediately got to work on its list of design imperatives. Toyota immediately went about understanding the people who would actually *purchase their product*—the U.S. market's luxury car buyers.

An Ability to Win analysis could have told VW that the Phaeton was not going to work, at least in its present form. It also would have pointed out how VW could have invested in critical capabilities that might have given the story a different ending.

TWO ABILITY TO WIN FREQUENTLY ASKED QUESTIONS

Clients are usually very intrigued by the Ability to Win analysis and typically have the following two questions about its use:

Question 1: Where do we get the type of information that goes into an Ability to Win analysis?

In addition to the tools and sources from previous chapters that we've mentioned, you can obtain much of the Ability to Win information through both formal and informal research.

In Chapter 2, we outlined an informal card sort technique that will help you not only understand customer values and benefits sought but also begin giving you ideas for the priority order that customers ascribe to each. This is one of many techniques that great marketers—along with their research partners, if you can afford one—employ constantly.

(*continued*)

(*continued*)

What's our proof that this is done all the time? Ask yourself, when was the last time you were asked to fill out a rating questionnaire of some sort? Probably in the last month—if not the last week!

The fact is that smart marketers are constantly involved in trying to get this type of insight from their customers. If you want an advantage, you must commit to constantly seeking insights. The Ability to Win tool gives you the most powerful guidance and format for analyzing this information and using it to create a powerful strategy.

Question 2: How do we know if we got the Ability to Win analysis "right"?

The Ability to Win is a scorecard of how well your company and competitors are meeting target market needs. As such, the scores should correlate with the actual marketplace situation. In other words, if you are the market share leader or laggard, your total Ability to Win scores in relation to your competitors should reflect that.

If you have modeled yourself against your two biggest competitors and both have larger market shares than you, then their scores should (in most cases) be higher. If your Ability to Win scores are higher than competitors who are achieving much higher shares, then you probably got something wrong, or it is illustrating that you are about to gain significant market share by better meeting customers' needs.

We passionately believe companies with a strong Ability to Win analysis have a huge advantage in the marketplace. They have a firm grasp on reality, even though it may not be a pretty picture in the first or second analysis. The good news is that the analysis serves as a launching pad for great strategies and value propositions that customers will love. The remaining chapters of this book will help you use your Ability to Win findings to create, communicate, and capture the full value of your offerings.

CHAPTER 7

The Magnetic Effect of Focus

Apple Demonstrates How Aiming at a Tight Target Leads to Massive Profits

POWER TOOL: STRATEGIC POSITION ANALYSIS (SPA)—A.K.A. THE PRIORITIZER

A person who aims at nothing is sure to hit it.

—Anonymous

FOCUS TO GROW

The phrase *focus to grow* has been our consulting firm's attention-getting tag-line for a number of years. It works because it is counterintuitive, is unusual, and addresses the hot-button issue of growth. People want to know how we propose to help them solve an apparent contradiction: finding growth in sales, as well as in profits, by *narrowing* focus and shooting at a tighter target.

The answer lies in extreme brand and product differentiation. The business world is overrun with me-too products that offer no apparent difference in value. Conversely, the most successful brands and products have legions of loy-alists who will gladly speak of the functional and emotional reasons for their continued patronage. Brands with a unique value proposition have an easier time growing.

Certainly, most strategists aim for differentiation. So why do so many end up missing the mark? In our experience, companies dilute their offerings by trying to be all things to all types of customers. They do not make brave choices about the segments or markets they will *not* serve.

Even if these companies create the needs-based segments we talked about in Chapter 3, they still make lukewarm tea because they try to serve all segments or markets in the pursuit of growth. In Chapter 5, we showed you how to model Enterprise's focus discipline using a simple tool called Segment Attractiveness. In Chapter 6, we introduced the versatile Ability to Win tool. Now, we will show you how to use both of these analyses to make *even better* focusing choices using a tool we call the Prioritizer. (Please note, out of deference to past clients who know this tool as the Strategic Position Analysis—or SPA—that we have used SPA and The Prioritizer interchangeably in this chapter.)

To paraphrase the famous quote of noted business author Michael Porter, "the essence of strategy is as much about what you will *not* do as it is about what you *will* do." The following chapter is about the courage to make choices and go all-in with a very unique offer to one or a few targets—and ignore the rest.

A courageous and insightful mind-set is what we found when reverse-engineering Apple's massive success. Although much has been written about Apple elsewhere, the approach we discovered has largely been overlooked in accounts of the company's success. You'll see what we mean as you read on, but what we call Apple's magnetic effect of focus is very evident if you know what to look for.

At this very moment, if you are in a public place, see how easy it is to find someone *outside* of Apple's target market using one of its products. Look for the opposite of a design-conscious, techy-looking countercultural rebel. For instance, as I (Tom) write this while sitting in a local Starbucks, I am looking at a 50-something-year-old man in a traditional suit and tie using his iPhone to conduct business. The iPhone model he is using looks to be the exact same one as the cool, Bohemian-looking 20-something guy having a conversation on the other side of the coffee shop is using.

What's the significance of this observation? When companies are so good at providing unique products or services to a tightly defined target market, they powerfully draw in customers from other segments *without* diluting their offer. They also have a deceptively simple and seldom practiced way of thinking about *how* to grow. This chapter will demonstrate the specific mind-set you need and a tool that you can use to "magnetize" your approach and gain significant top- and bottom-line growth through focus.

LOOKING FOR GROWTH IN ALL OF THE WRONG PLACES

The following scene could have taken place in any one of dozens of workshops we've conducted for Fortune 500 clients over the past decade. A brand team had just done a very thorough job of analyzing its customer segments, each segment's attractiveness (see Chapter 5), and their brand's ability to win (see Chapter 6) with each.

Combining these two analyses and also estimating the revenue potential for each segment (denoted by the size of each circle shown in Figure 7.1), the team created a version of the featured tool for this chapter.

The Prioritizer allows teams to look at a lot of information at one time. They can see how their segments and markets map out onto a grid that ultimately analyzes their best and worst opportunities for growth.

The *y*-axis measures Segment or Market Attractiveness (the scores come from the work you would have done in Chapter 5). The *x*-axis plots Ability to Win (the scores for this axis come from the previous chapter).

Each segment is plotted based on their scores. Segment A would have scored 900 for attractiveness and 700 for ability to win.

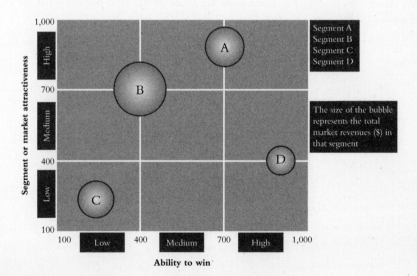

Figure 7.1   Strategic Position Analysis: The Prioritizer™

In this illustration, segment A is highly attractive, and the company completing the analysis has a strong ability to win. Contrast this with segment C, which has a low attractiveness and low ability is win.

The brand team that produced this Prioritizer had come a long way in just a day and a half. Before the workshop, the team saw their target market as a single group of customers, all with similar needs. In a very short time, they had not only segmented their market into smaller groups with different needs but were also able to use the Segment Attractiveness and Ability to Win tools to develop an entirely new way of looking at their strategic options.

Now it was time to make a significant marketing strategy decision about how much time and resource to expend against each segment. Their answer: "We'll spend 25 percent of our time and resources on each of the four segments."

WHAT?!

How could intelligent people who had just conducted such a thorough analysis be *so wrong?* How could a reasonable person justify spending *any* resources on segment C in the Prioritizer in Figure 7.1, a very unattractive segment in which the brand had a very low ability to win? Every dollar of resource spent on segment C takes away a potential investment in further extending their position with segment A, or improving the brand's ability to win with the very large segment B.

The team decided not to play the sound strategic game that the Prioritizer can help direct. Used correctly, the tool leads to an allocation of resources toward the brand's best opportunities, seeking to create unique value for one or a few target segments.

Unfortunately, the team eschewed all the work on segmentation, attractiveness, and ability to win it had done. It was as though they had never attended the session and instead opted to spread its resource across all of its different types of customers, which ultimately provides unique value for *none of them*.

This brand team's approach—to seek growth at all costs—was their major problem. They believed that ignoring *any* segment was, in effect, losing a prospective opportunity to grow the top line. The notion of "growth at all costs" has been beaten into most strategists' brains; it seems almost immoral, in a business sense, to walk away from any potential opportunity to sell more.

THE MAGNETIC MIND-SET

Stewards of great brands think very differently than the average market strategist. They understand a powerful principle of growth that's best illustrated in the chart depicted in Figure 7.2 (originally developed by our friends and colleagues Don Peppers and Martha Rogers of Peppers and Rogers Group).

We call this concept the *magnetic mind-set*. Companies that practice it can find growth ideas without diluting their focus. Ultimately, this approach leads to such unique value propositions that customers from nontarget segments are drawn to the companies' offers, *without the company having to specifically appeal to that segment.*

Typically, companies operate in the horizontal dimension of Figure 7.2, seeking growth by trying to find new customers, segments, and/or markets for *existing* products. This seems like the logical, and maybe only, way to grow. It also explains why the workshop clients described in the previous scenario couldn't seem to find a segment of customers that they would *not* pursue.

In order to appeal to new customer segments, companies usually have to dilute their offerings and provide different (often lower) pricing. Upscale brands try to appeal to the budget-conscious segment and vice versa. In Chapter 6, Mercedes-Benz tried to move downscale to appeal to more mainstream car owners with the A-Class. This led Volkswagen to try to move upscale with the Phaeton.

Movement along the customers reached axis in Figure 7.2 puts tremendous pressure on profit margins—and being able to reach these new segments often requires different skills and expertise than a company currently possesses.

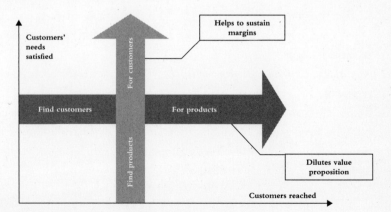

Figure 7.2   The Magnetic Mind-Set

Source: Reprinted with permission from Peppers and Rogers Group, www.1to1media.com.

Conversely, magnetic marketers operate in the vertical dimension. Their growth comes from a mind-set of *finding more products for their existing target customers.* They will look to leverage what they already know about their target to create value and drive growth, capitalizing on what they already do well. Moving along the customer needs satisfied axis in this way usually helps sustain and sometimes even improve margins while expanding sales.

The following three case studies show both types of mind-sets in action. The first looks at a company (Iridium) that's reemerging from a huge loss to reap the benefits of a magnetic mind-set approach and grow through focus. The second shows how a company (BlackBerry) that had an enviable marketplace position lost it in just a few short years from an apparent lack of focus. And the third shows how Apple has, until very recently, embodied this magnetic effect of focus better than any company we can think of.

Special thanks to our European Partner, Sean Welham, who developed the cases that follow.

A TALE OF THREE COMMUNICATIONS COMPANIES

All three of the companies profiled here participate in the high-tech telecommunications industry. Three different market segments from this industry can be described as follows:

1. *Market A: Business smartphone users:* This is a sizable market, especially when considering add-on and adjacent products that can be cross-sold to business users.
2. *Market B: Consumer smartphone users:* This is a massively large-sized segment.
3. *Market C: Global must-have communicators:* This market is defined as people who need secure communications in areas that have limited, traditional cell phone infrastructure (e.g., military personnel in Afghanistan). This is a relatively small market.

Note that the sizes of these segments do not change as each company analyzes them; however, the attractiveness and their ability to win changes based on the company's perspective.

Each case includes a unique Prioritizer that hypothesizes the way each company may have looked at these three potential markets.

Iridium Gets It Right—The Second Time Around

Satellite phone communications company Iridium wanted to rule the traveling businessperson mobile phone market—and its founders thought they had the right approach to do it. In the 1990s, communications satellites orbited at more than 22,000 miles from the Earth's surface. At the time, mobile callers had to use very large phones and engage in frustrating conversations due to quarter-second voice delays.

Iridium's idea was to employ 66 low-Earth-orbiting (LEO) satellites that would facilitate mobile calls from *any* global location, resulting in smaller phones and imperceptible voice delays. This would be great for the rapidly growing global business traveler market and would provide the company with a base to possibly pursue even larger mobile communications markets.

Unfortunately, Iridium made a serious miscalculation.

The company assumed that the build-out of Earth-based cellular phone infrastructure would be much slower than it actually was. Over the 11 years of Iridium's prelaunch development, even smaller cell phones with better reception became widely available. The Iridium business unit—part of the Motorola Corporation—had already launched its LEO satellites, but the product was dead on arrival. The company lost huge sums and filed for Chapter 11 bankruptcy.

But there may yet be a happy ending to the Iridium story. The business unit reorganized to try to salvage the investment in the LEO satellites. Iridium discovered a small niche that the company could serve uniquely, which some call the global must-have communications market. Examples of this market include the military command-and-control personnel in isolated places such as Afghanistan that we mentioned earlier or managers of manufacturing plants in remote regions not yet covered by cell towers.

Serving these markets has helped Iridium reemerge as a viable entity with more than 100,000 subscribers. But ongoing success in high-tech markets requires constant evolution. As the company considers its growth options, will it be tempted once again to take on the established players and carve out a part of the larger, more lucrative business smartphone segment? A Prioritizer, such as the one shown in Figure 7.3, would underscore the danger to the company in trying to find more customers for its existing products.

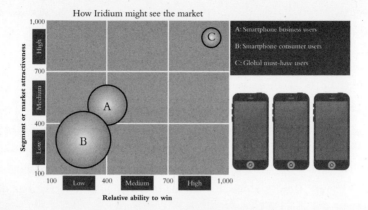

Figure 7.3   Strategic Position Analysis: Iridium

Source: Copyright © 2014. Impact Planning Group. All rights reserved.

The hypothesized, fictitious Strategic Position Analysis (SPA) in this figure shows that although the business smartphone market is reasonably attractive to Iridium, it's not one that it is well equipped to serve. The powerful cellular players in the market, who are still building out global mobile phone networks, have a huge existing advantage.

But how do you find growth opportunities with a segment as small as market C? If you have the magnetic mind-set discussed earlier, you try to find *more products to sell* to your customers instead of pursuing more customers for existing products. Fortunately for Iridium investors, this appears to be exactly what the company is doing.

Specifically, Iridium recently launched its next generation of satellites that will enable it to be a leader in the machine-to-machine (MTM) communications that many of its global must-have military and manufacturing users want. As the moniker implies, MTM allows machines to communicate with one another and make preprogrammed and user-directed adjustments to optimize operations. It also provides benefits such as enabling pallets and packages to communicate their location to shippers, in addition to a range of military intelligence capabilities.

This type of approach seems to suggest that Iridium gets it when it comes to the magnetic mind-set.

BlackBerry Loses a Powerful, Lucrative Position

BlackBerry's early focus on enabling mobile e-mail endeared the company to the massive segment of on-the-go businesspeople. Such was the devotion of BlackBerry users that it was dubbed the CrackBerry in the United States (a reference to the addictive qualities of crack cocaine). An investment in the company's stock in 2003, just as it was adding phone call capabilities and Web browsing to its devices, would have returned an astonishing 6,600 percent return if sold at its peak in 2008.

Unfortunately, the stock price has returned to below $10—levels not seen since 2003—amidst extreme struggles to hold onto its once-envied brand equity. What happened?

It is no coincidence that BlackBerry's stock price hit its peak just after the introduction of Apple's iPhone. As BlackBerry strategized how to combat what looked like a significant, direct challenge to its business, the company likely saw its market opportunities as shown in Figure 7.4.

Sadly, rather than protect its great position in the business smartphone market, BlackBerry made the rueful decision to pursue more customers for its products. It attempted to appeal to consumer users (market B) by introducing personal-use-featured phones like the BlackBerry Storm and the Pearl.

But the iPhone entry had heightened the perception of the cell phone as a personal fashion accessory, something very different from BlackBerry's more functional, business-like persona. Not only did BlackBerry fail to gain traction in the consumer market, but it diverted its focus and ultimately lost a significant share of the business smartphone market as well. It squandered an incredibly valuable position—a product that its affluent users once considered not only valued but *addictive*.

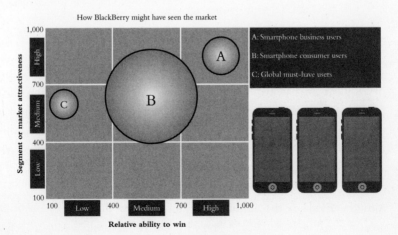

Figure 7.4   Strategic Position Analysis: BlackBerry

Instead of trying to find more customers for their existing products, BlackBerry could have developed and offered more products for their loyal business customer base.

Consider the following: Clayton Christiansen, esteemed author of *The Innovator's Dilemma,* cowrote an intriguing article about segmentation for *MIT Sloan Management Review* titled "Finding the Right Job for Your Product." In it, Christiansen laments the lack of creative thinking in business that drives big ideas.

Christiansen and his collaborators claim that the automotive industry has missed a big idea—a car designed to serve as a mobile office. Built with technological connectivity, flexible workspace, multiple electronics charging stations, and so on, the car would help its large target market complete an important job: be more efficient when an automobile is a worker's "base of operations."

And who would have been a great technology partner for an automotive company for such a design? Why BlackBerry, of course—who also could have focused on creating additional applications and services that made it indispensible to its addicted customer base. It could have concentrated on enabling better audio conferencing, easier document sharing, integrating text messaging functionality—business communication and productivity ideas that other companies have subsequently capitalized on.

Had the company been more focused on developing new products like this for its existing customers, rather than trying to sell more smartphones to a consumer market, it would likely still own its once-powerful position with their target market.

Apple Magnetically Attracts BlackBerry's Customers—Without Really Trying

Historically, Apple has avoided the temptation to overreach when creating gadgets for its design-conscious, simplicity-seeking, different-thinking technology customers. Apple's post-2000s success has been about nothing else but *finding new technology* products for this segment, rather than trying to find new customers for its products. They are the magnetic mind-set personified.

From the iPod, to the iPhone and the iPad, to the rumored products the press has dubbed the iWatch and iTV (an Apple-designed smart television), the company under Steve Jobs was continuously looking to leverage its strengths in design and simplicity to find products that its target segment loves and pays a premium for. This approach has allowed Apple to grow well outside of its target segment and still be widely thought of as a growth company capable of 20+ percent quarterly growth in sales and profits—despite being a mature entity.

Given what's been written about Steve Jobs, it's difficult to imagine him using an SPA—or any tools—to drive his strategy. He is an example of a rare genius who just knew what to do—and whose vision, independence of thought, and uncompromising nature led a company to significantly change the business landscape.

But this book is about trying to reengineer genius strategies so that you can duplicate them uniquely in your own industry. So let's imagine for a moment how Jobs and his team at Apple *might* have built a Prioritizer to analyze opportunities in the smartphone market as they were designing the iPhone (Figure 7.5).

Like an eclipse, Apple's mono-focus on the consumer smartphone market (B in Figure 7.5) obscured any thought of seeing, considering, or reaching for any other segment or market. The iPhone design was characteristic of Jobs's product development: exacting, uncompromising, and targeted at the typical Apple customer.

The iPhone—and the next Apple mega-hit, the iPad—were *not* designed to enable any specific business functionality. Jobs would not have compromised

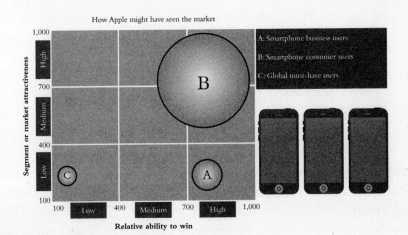

Figure 7.5   Strategic Position Analysis: Apple

any iPhone features to make sure it also worked well with company e-mail intranets and networks.

So what happened? The iPhone became so popular that business users, and many others outside of Apple's consumer target segment, began to desire it. Technology companies like Aruba Networks successfully scrambled to create interoperability hardware and software to allow individuals to use their iPhones at work. Developers and information technology (IT) managers created applications that delivered further business functionality for iPhones.

A similar phenomenon took shape with the iPad. Entrepreneurs and company IT personnel, *not Apple employees,* developed applications that allowed their sales reps to use Apple's tablet more productively. Today, many employees use iPads instead of bulky laptops to make flexible, customized, winning presentations anywhere, anytime. Statements from current Apple chief executive officer Tim Cook seem to suggest that even the brand itself was surprised by the magnitude of iPad business use.

The magnetic effect of focus *does* pleasantly surprise practitioners with unexpected growth—while shocking and maddening competitors.

The result of Apple's focus in the smartphone market flummoxed the entire industry. Even today, you can find YouTube vignettes that mock Apple customers' blind devotion to the iPhone despite some considerable functionality differences in competitive smartphones.

That all seems like sour grapes when you look at the facts. There's no denying that the iPhone almost single-handedly cured previous BlackBerry users of their powerful CrackBerry addiction and became the new designer drug of choice. As a result, Apple now owns a significant share of a market *it didn't target.*

WWJD? (WHAT WOULD JOBS DO?)

As of this writing, there is a popular buzz that Apple will launch a low-cost iPhone to appeal to the masses, including China's emerging middle class. This would be a significant departure from the mind-set that's been such a part of Apple's long-term success and is more akin to the find new customers for existing products overreaching that we see all too often from companies out of Apple's league.

Had Steve Jobs still been at the helm, this notion would have been quickly—and, in true Jobs's style, mockingly—dismissed. Those hoping for a mass-market entry may be reacting to the recent retreat of Apple's stock price, as well as the company's slowing growth and declining earnings.

Our long-term prognosis for Apple's success in a low-cost iPhone market is not good. We are sympathetic to Tim Cook and the company's executive leadership, who must be under enormous pressure from the company's various stakeholders to duplicate the magic of Jobs's leadership and the consistent, exponential top-line increases. You may be feeling similar pressures in your own business—although likely not as extreme or as public.

But there is another path to growth, the one that we've highlighted continuously in this chapter. With exciting products like the iWatch and iTV on Apple's drawing board—which represent more of the find products for customers approach of the Jobs era—we think the company will fare better if it can forget about the mass market and be patient until these new ventures are ready for launch.

THE MAGNETIC EFFECT OF FOCUS

We can summarize the mind-set we've discussed in this chapter as follows:

- Focus narrowly on a target market or one or two segments. Make a *truly differentiating offer* that speaks so specifically and uniquely to your targets' needs that it incites fierce, margin-proof loyalty and magnetically attracts those outside of the immediate target, without watering down the value proposition. If your capabilities allow, you can create separate, highly targeted offers to a few segments, à la Quidel (see Chapter 3).
- When you need to find new sources of growth, consider the mind-set of creating more products for your target customers, rather than wooing more customers for your products.

This formula and mind-set can provide an infinite source of ideas and strategies. It can also seem more like swimming downstream, because it often leverages the capabilities and skills that your company already possesses.

A TOOL TO HELP CREATE THE MAGNETIC EFFECT OF FOCUS: THE PRIORITIZER™

The Prioritizer is perhaps the simplest or our tools to construct, especially if you have completed a Segment or Market Attractiveness analysis (as detailed in Chapter 5) and Ability to Win analysis (as detailed in Chapter 6) for the same segments or markets. Several of our previous illustrations in this chapter show that the SPA is a cross-mapping of these two analyses.

Because you probably already get the idea of how the analysis is put together, we'll focus here on some of the finer points in constructing the SPA. Then we will close with one final admonition regarding the mindset to properly create focus and gain all of the resulting benefits.

ADD ONE OR MORE COMPETITORS' POSITION TO YOUR SPA

In Figure 7.6 we've repeated the first SPA from this chapter with the addition of a plot showing the competitive position for one competitor in each segment. It helps immensely to understand how you stand in comparison to one or two of your most important competitors when making focus decisions.

This is relatively easy to do, because the Ability to Win analysis in the previous chapter included a score for at least two competitors. However, the other SPA input, Segment Attractiveness analysis (from Chapter 5), did *not* include an analysis for your competitors.

You have two options for completing your SPA competitive plot(s):

Option A: Assume competitors feel the same attractiveness toward a segment or market as you do. The example shown in Figure 7.6 makes this assumption, with the competitive plot for each segment being on the same horizontal plane as your own plot. Keep in mind that is not the most accurate option, because your competitors likely have a different attractiveness formula than you do. Nonetheless, this saves you a lot of time and delivers most of the value you seek from the SPA, pointing out your best opportunities to focus and grow.

Option B: Complete a Segment Attractiveness analysis as you believe your competitors would. This is time-consuming and requires a level of competitor intelligence that may be difficult to source. However, it can be a really useful path for getting inside your competitors' heads and predicting how hard (or not) they will fight for certain markets or segments. This adds a level of sophistication to your analysis and resulting strategic moves that would not be as clear when utilizing only option A.

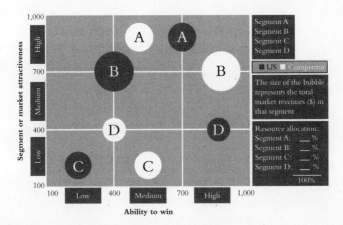

Figure 7.6   The Prioritizer™
Source: Copyright © 2014. Impact Planning Group. All rights reserved.

Adding one or more competitors to the SPA can enhance your strategy's insight and sophistication. You can see in the example how placing significant focus on segment B will require that you go head to head with a competitor who obviously is already delivering significant value to the segment. Should you invest to catch up in segment B, or place more investment in segment A, where you have a competitive advantage? The competitor SPA plot keeps you from making ill-informed decisions and missing important opportunities.

WHEN YOU HAVE COMPLETED YOUR SPA(S), MAKE A RESOURCE ALLOCATION DECISION

As we discussed earlier in this chapter, the reason to complete this analysis is to force a decision about where to focus your resources. The

(continued)

(continued)

SEGMENT A:	____%
SEGMENT B:	____%
SEGMENT C:	____%
SEGMENT D:	____%
	100%

Figure 7.7   Resource Allocation

resource box in the bottom right-hand corner of the SPA at the beginning of this section is repeated in Figure 7.7.

We hope that you will not do what the client team profiled at the beginning of this chapter did: ignore the results and spread your resources evenly across the four segments! *Be bold*. Practice a focus mind-set, unevenly allocate your resources, and then get creative about finding new products and services for your target markets and segments.

You may be wondering how, once you've decided where to focus, to uncover these creative ideas that will fulfill your target market's needs like no other company. Keep reading: the remainder of the chapters in this book will give you examples and tools for creating innovative, relevant offers and powerful approaches for communicating and capturing the full value of those offers!

CHAPTER 8

Viva la Differentiation

Three Differentiation Strategies, Including How Nike Convinced Us That Sneakers Are a Fashion Item

POWER TOOLS: DIFFERENTIAL ADVANTAGE WITH FUTURE STATE ABILITY TO WIN

Life is either a daring adventure, or nothing.
> —Helen Keller, American author, political activist, and lecturer

OUR OWN COMPANY'S SEARCH FOR DIFFERENTIATION

On a pleasant summer evening at an Italian restaurant, we sat around the dinner table listening intently. It was the night before our consulting firm's annual two-day strategy meetings, and we had asked one of our guests "the question."

It's our tradition to invite special guests—a mix of customers and strategic partners—to the dinners before our annual meetings. It's one way to gain market insights that guide our strategic discussions. Tonight, Ginny, a human resources professional who had experienced our consulting firm's work while employed at General Electric, was on the hot seat.

Ginny was now an independent consultant, and we often worked with her on marketing engagements that involved leadership development and significant organizational change. The question we asked her that night was: *What benefits does our firm deliver to clients who work with us?*

131

After thinking for just a moment, Ginny replied, "When companies do marketing planning, they go through a process, check off all of the boxes, and think they are done. But then if anyone asks them, 'What are you providing to customers that is different than what your competitors deliver?'. . . they get this panicked look in their eyes. Your company helps them to *find that difference.*"

Eureka! In a single statement, Ginny had helped us find a new way to describe our firm's value proposition: we help companies of all types *be different* from their competitors.

We believe that being meaningfully different—creating differentiation—is the *very reason* for the existence of the marketing function itself. If customers don't perceive any difference at all among products in a category, they usually choose the lowest-priced product or service. Marketing plays a very limited role in a price war.

But people buy products that aren't the lowest priced all the time. And this is because they perceive that the higher-priced product or service has some explicit or inherent advantage, a difference, that warrants a higher price. Developing this difference is marketing's primary job.

Differentiation strategies can come from many different aspects of a strong marketing plan. Indeed, our previous chapters have shown you how you can distinguish your products by finding new, underserved stakeholders, or uncovering unspoken customer benefits sought, or segmenting creatively, or targeting specifically with discipline.

But now you have reached the point in the marketing process when you are ready to get very specific about differentiation strategies. Whether you are ahead or behind in your Ability to Win, you can't stand still. You are about to learn three powerful ways to uncover strategies that allow your company to stand out among your competitors and gain higher sales and profits. Viva la differentiation!

INNOVATE TO DIFFERENTIATE: THREE STRATEGIES THAT EMANATE FROM YOUR ABILITY TO WIN ANALYSIS

You may be wondering how the concept of differentiation compares with another hot topic in business today: innovation. Differentiation in marketing is the act of *proving* to customers that a product or service has an *important difference* when compared with competitors. Innovation without differentiation—that is, new inventions that don't meet customer needs *better* than existing products—have limited or no commercial value.

RIM invented and introduced the Z10 BlackBerry model that provided a new operating system, design, and touch screen; however, it wasn't perceived as that different (or better) than other mobile devices on the market. We often see this with our industrial clients that tell us, "We invented something new that we are about to launch; however, it is a me-too in our category."

Differentiation adds an external, customer-focused angle to innovations. Rather than seeking to innovate in a vacuum, or solely for the sake of doing something new, companies should innovate to differentiate. The tools you now have, culminating in the Ability to Win analysis you completed in Chapter 6, provide a superior foundation to think about how you will differentiate your product powerfully.

Figure 8.1 is our Differential Advantage framework, which will uncover plenty of innovate to differentiate strategies to consider. You can then analyze each of the strategies generated to find the most powerful ones, using this chapter's featured tool, the Future State Ability to Win.

We will now illustrate each of these strategies through case studies.

Strategy 1: Similar Tactics

Our advice is to examine Similar Tactics differentiation approaches first because they are the most straightforward and typically take less time and resources

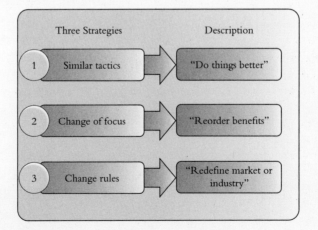

Figure 8.1 The Differential Advantage Framework

to implement. Rather than the more adventurous strategies we'll cover later, this one simply requires that you uncover customers' most pressing needs and deliver on them better than the competition does (see Figure 8.2).

Specifically, you look for the two to three benefits sought in your Ability to Win chart that have the highest weights. You then narrow your focus to the critical capabilities where the ratings show that *no competitor has a clear advantage*. Can you significantly improve your market position by enhancing your capabilities—or your customer perceptions—in these areas?

A Medical Diagnostics Device Company Uses Similar Tactics to Win with Hospitals One client of ours who sold computed tomography (CT) scan and magnetic resonance imaging (MRI) equipment to hospitals used the similar tactics approach to quickly differentiate themselves in an intensely competitive market.

Our client's ability to win, which we'll call the current state to reflect their situation *before* their differentiation strategies, showed that they were lagging behind two competitors in a tightly contested market (Figure 8.3).

When the client looked at the ratings associated with the top three most highly weighted benefits, our client realized that *no company,* including themselves, was setting themselves apart in the minds of customers, as evidenced by all scores being similar.

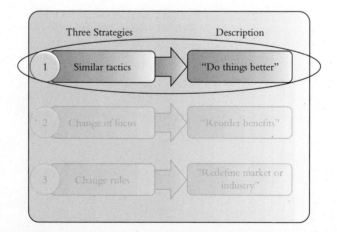

Figure 8.2   The Differential Advantage Framework: Strategy 1

Benefit Sought	Benefit Weight	Critical Capability	CC Weight	Our Client		Competitor A		Competitor B	
				Rating (1-10)	Score	Rating (1-10)	Score	Rating (1-10)	Score
New and Improved Clinical Applications	30	Better Patient Outcomes	15	7	105	7	105	6	90
		Breakthrough Apps	15	6	90	7	105	6	90
Better Imaging	25	Innovative Tech	15	6	90	7	105	6	90
		Software	10	5	50	5	50	6	60
Streamlined Operations	20	Process Efficiency	10	5	50	5	50	5	50
		Consulting	10	4	40	5	50	3	30
Funding for Research Grants	15	Link to Grant Providers	10	4	40	5	50	8	80
		Biz Case Help	5	2	10	3	15	2	10
Organizational Recognition	10	Peer Forums	5	3	15	5	25	4	20
		Media Connections	5	3	15	5	25	5	25
	100		100	Total	505	Total	580	Total	545

Figure 8.3   Current State Ability to Win: Diagnostics Imaging Market

Source: Copyright © 2014. Impact Planning Group. All rights reserved.

Further to their analysis, no company was doing a good job at addressing customer needs. A score of 500 can be interpreted as meeting only 50 percent of the customers' needs. A score of 700 or 800 (i.e., 70 percent to 80 percent) would indicate a much stronger ability.

Unfortunately, our client did not have any significant innovations in their research and development (R&D) pipeline that would help them improve their ratings in the first two technology-driven benefit areas noted in Figure 8.3. So what could management do to differentiate?

They were surprised to see how important it was becoming for hospitals to find ways to cut costs through streamlining operations. With a weighting of "20," it was the third most important benefit sought in their Ability to Win chart. *Here* was an area to which our client could add some value.

The client team had studied the steps hospital personnel take *after* capturing a diagnostic image and had specifically engineered their machines to help make this process faster and more efficient. But communication about these process-enhancing features had gotten lost. Instead, our client's sales and marketing messages focused on other, more technological features.

By placing more focus on their marketing communications about the superior process efficiencies their machines enabled, our client would quickly be able to improve hospital's perceptions in this area. In addition, they learned from the Ability to Win chart that their hospital customers cared about best practices consulting. They wanted any help they could get in running a more efficient, streamlined diagnostics department.

The company had more of these types of resources internally than they were using.

To model whether these two strategies would make a difference in their markets, they used a tool called the *Future State Ability to Win*. This modifies the Current State Ability to Win by changing weightings, ratings, and scores from pursuing various differential advantage strategies.

Figure 8.4 is our client's Future State Ability to Win. The shaded areas indicate the rating and score changes from the two strategies (originally these scores were 5 and 4). The new scores of 9 and 8 indicate the perceptual scores the company believed it could achieve from segment customers if they made the appropriate investment and focus on these two critical capabilities.

Benefit Sought	Benefit Weight	Critical Capability	CC Weight	Our Client		Competitor A		Competitor B	
				Rating (1-10)	Score	Rating (1-10)	Score	Rating (1-10)	Score
New and Improved Clinical Applications	30	Better Patient Outcomes	15	7	105	7	105	6	90
		Breakthrough apps	15	6	90	7	105	6	90
Better Imaging	25	Innovative Tech	15	6	90	7	105	6	90
		Software	10	5	50	5	50	6	60
Streamlined Operations	20	Process Efficiency	10	9	90	5	50	5	50
		Consulting	10	8	80	5	50	3	30
Funding for Research Grants	15	Link to Grant Providers	10	4	40	5	50	8	80
		Biz Case Help	5	2	10	3	15	2	10
Organizational Recognition	10	Peer Forums	5	3	15	5	25	4	20
		Media Connections	5	3	15	5	25	5	25
	100		100	Total	585	Total	580	Total	545

Ability to Win Score
Increased from 505 to 585

Figure 8.4   Future State Ability to Win: Diagnostics Imaging Market

You can see when comparing the total Future State Ability to Win with the Current State how the similar tactics strategies moved our client's total score from being third among competitors to first. The strategy worked—and the company began to gain market share in the segment almost immediately.

Strategy 2: Changing the Focus

After looking for similar tactics approaches, marketers should next seek opportunities to *modify their target customers' focus.* Companies use this strategy to reorder benefits—literally, change customers' minds—to alter which ones they consider most important (see Figure 8.5).

Changing people's minds is one of the hardest things to do, in life *and* in business. Nonetheless, some companies have changed the minds of an entire culture. A great example of this is Nike.

Reverse-Engineering Nike's Success in Changing Customers' Focus Like Dell and Apple, much has been written about Nike's road to success. Rather than rehash the deep details, we'll give a brief summary of the athletic shoe market at the time, and use our tools to explain what happened.

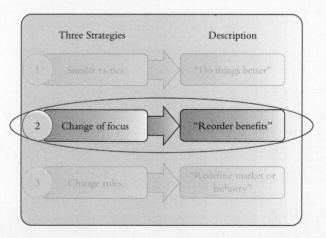

Figure 8.5   The Differential Advantage Framework: Strategy 2

A Brief History of the Early Days of the "Sneaker Wars" Nike made its initial big impact on the world in the 1980s. The exercise craze had yet to take hold among adults in the previous decades, so the primary target market for sneakers were children and teenagers. The typical buyer was a parent. In most cases, moms, with minimal input from their children, would purchase athletic shoes for their sons and daughters to use in gym class and in sports.

The biggest sneaker brands at the time were Keds, PF Flyers, and Chuck Taylor Converse All-Stars. Parents decided which to buy based on whether the shoes had a reputation for being comfortable and whether they were readily available at their local shoe store in the right color and size.

PF Flyers had a position based loosely on better athletic performance (PF stood for Perfect Foundation), but no brand was really pushing the envelope on this angle. The only real fashion-oriented need in the category was the desire to match school colors as closely as possible.

We've hypothesized what a simplified Current State Ability to Win analysis (excluding critical capabilities) for the athletic shoe market might have looked like at this time (Figure 8.6).

As you can see in Figure 8.6, the top two highly weighted benefits sought, be comfortable and find what I need, reflect parents' main concerns at the time.

Note the low-weight for be cool; this illustrates the concept that there was very little fashion-oriented consideration in the category at the time. Certainly, many teenagers had a lot to say about the *other* apparel items parents purchased for them. But unlike with clothes, parents just didn't face a lot of pressure to buy specific—and expensive—athletic shoes prior to the 1980s.

However, this was about to change.

Segment: Teenager Athletic Shoes		Keds		PF Flyers		Converse	
Benefit Sought	Benefit Weight	Rating (1-10)	Score	Rating (1-10)	Score	Rating (1-10)	Score
Be Comfortable	50	6	300	8	400	7	350
Find What I Need	30	8	240	6	180	9	270
Perform Better	15	5	75	7	105	5	75
Be Cool	5	5	25	5	25	5	25
	100	Total	640	Total	710	Total	720

Figure 8.6   Current State Ability to Win: Pre-1980s Athletic Shoes

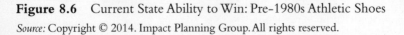
Source: Copyright © 2014. Impact Planning Group. All rights reserved.

Reebok's Strong Move into Aerobics Cause Nike to Seek an Emotional Connection with Customers As the fitness craze blossomed in the 1980s, companies such as Nike, Reebok, and Adidas emerged. Looking to take share from the established brands, all these new brands saw a big opportunity to differentiate on the benefit sought of perform better. They focused on using science and technology to design lighter, more comfortable, durable shoes that could help exercisers log many miles.

The Nike brand was very focused on performance. Founder, ex-Oregon track star Phil Knight, along with cofounder Bill Bowerman, Knight's world-renowned track coach during his days at Oregon, wanted to create the best running shoes on the market.

So it had to hurt when, in the early 1980s, Reebok had gained a better performance perception in the market by developing a shoe specifically designed for the growing aerobics craze.

Demonstrating a competitive zeal that was to become legendary, Nike was not willing to cede category leadership of athletic shoes to Reebok. The Nike management team likely considered several options for combat. Nike could compete with Reebok directly on a performance basis, or it could find a different path to gain an upper hand. Betting on a personal theory, Knight and Nike took a more indirect route, one that brilliantly tapped into the teenage instinct for belonging.

Nike Changes the Focus from Performance to Fashion Knight decided to establish Nike by making its brand about the *individuals wearing* the shoes. The personal theory driving this approach was what he called the Five Cool Guys.

Knight believed that there were generally about five cool guys that set the standards for what to wear in high schools. If Nike could duplicate the theory on a global scale, finding the five coolest athletes to wear and endorse Nike, teenagers would want to associate with the brand.

Demonstrating a firm grasp of its market, the company sought endorsements from successful-but-rebellious athletes. Four big names fit this profile: Steve Prefontaine, John McEnroe, Andre Agassi, and Charles Barkley were all controversial *and* successful. Each was, most likely, not too popular with old-school moms and dads, which made them even more attractive to many teenagers.

But it was the fifth cool guy on this list that lit a fire underneath the strategy. Michael Jordan was a basketball player who skipped the final year of his collegiate career at North Carolina (where he wore Converse shoes) to turn professional with the Chicago Bulls in 1984.

Having played for a very conservative coach in college, Nike knew that Jordan's super-human athletic skills, personality, and drive could turn him into a mega-superstar in the more free-flowing professional game. They took a chance and signed him to an endorsement contract *before* his first pro season, compensating him similarly to what Converse was paying already-proven stars like Magic Johnson.

The gamble paid off. After a season in which Jordan won the NBA rookie of the year award and led the league in gravity-defying moves, Jordan's popularity with the younger demographic was positively off the charts. So Nike decided to go forward with another big Michael Jordan bet.

With Reebok more focused on aerobics and with Converse doing very little to capitalize on the personality and charisma of the talented but more classically skilled Johnson, Nike released a shoe *named after* their new spokesperson. Paying homage to Jordan's ability to seemingly hang in the air forever, Nike released its Air Jordan shoes in 1985.

Several factors added to the allure of Air Jordans. For one, many critics noted that Jordan's team made the playoffs in his rookie year but were immediately eliminated. His flashy play turned off many traditionalists who noted that Magic Johnson had led his team to a championship in his first year. This endeared Jordan even more to young people, a demographic that has a long history of love affairs with nontraditionalists, including Elvis and the Beatles.

Oddly, the *high* price of Air Jordan shoes also added to their appeal. The shoe retailed for $65, at a time when Converse All-Stars cost around $25. At more than 2.5 times the price, teenagers could gain the additional pleasure of hearing their parents complain about how much Air Jordans cost.

Soon, many more than just the five coolest guys at every high school wanted to "be like Mike" (that renowned tagline from a Gatorade ad campaign featuring Jordan). As with many fashion items, the Nike swoosh logo on Air Jordans became a symbol of a certain status for teenagers.

Nike sold $130 million worth of Air Jordans in 1985 alone. The company exploded to $1 billion in sales in 1986 and never looked back. It has become a full-range athletic apparel marketer with a brand that signifies both athletic success and fashion.

Despite its roots as a performance-oriented brand, Nike consistently ranks at the top of *fashion brand* ratings among young people today. And the catalyst of it all was the Five Cool Guys strategy.

Reordering the Benefits = Changing Customers' Minds Nike accomplished a strategy we call reordering benefits. Simply put, Nike convinced teenagers that being cool should be higher on their list of benefits sought when buying athletic shoes than it was. By establishing the brand as it did, Nike showed them how to get something *every* teenager wants: a sense of belonging through wearing the Nike logo.

Parents of teenagers in the mid-1980s certainly felt this change of focus. Instead of the minimal stress they felt when buying athletic shoes before the Nike era, they now faced the enormous pressure from their teenagers to buy Nikes, at significantly higher prices than they were used to.

If Nike had been using an Ability to Win analysis to craft its strategy, you can see in Figure 8.7 how it probably would have viewed the opportunity to change the focus and reorder benefits in the sneaker industry.

Note: In the following Future State Ability to Win, we have removed the lowest-rated brand (Keds) from the previous Current State Ability to Win and replaced them with Reebok and Nike. Furthermore, we have hypothesized the customer perception ratings that Reebok and Nike would likely earn in the various benefits sought areas, keeping Converse and PF Flyers ratings constant.

Segment: Teenager Athletic Shoes		PF Flyers		Converse		Reebok		Nike	
Benefit Sought	Benefit Weight	Rating (1-10)	Score	Rating (1-10)	Score	Rating (1-10)	Score	Rating (1-10)	Score
Be Comfortable	20	8	160	7	140	7	140	7	140
Find What I Need	20	6	120	9	180	7	140	7	140
Perform Better	30	7	210	5	150	9	270	8	240
Be Cool	30	5	150	5	150	7	210	9	270
	100	Total	640	Total	620	Total	760		790

Reorder benefits to focus on perform better and be cool

Figure 8.7 Future State Ability to Win: How Nike May Have Seen the Athletic Shoe Opportunity

Source: Copyright © 2014. Impact Planning Group. All rights reserved.

Most important, we have highlighted how the new athletic shoe companies changed the focus to performance—and especially how Nike's marketing changed the focus to fashion and being cool. This is signified on an Ability to Win chart by a change in how customers view the benefit weights. Be comfortable and find what I need became much less important; perform better and be cool increased importance. More simply put, Nike *changed* our minds about what was important in athletic shoes and benefited from the strategy to become the market leader.

As you can see, Nike and Reebok both did well, with Reebok no doubt benefiting from Nike's success in growing the market. You also have to give credit to Reebok for being a strong catalyst for Nike's approach.

The lesson from Nike is that *it is possible to change customers' minds.* But it's not just about convincing customers to value what your company is good at.

Nike's reorientation strategy worked because it appealed to teenagers' innate sense of wanting to belong. The company was changing the category focus toward a strong emotional need *that already existed but was unmet* in its target market. This is why Nike was—and *is*—so successful.

Strategy 3: Changing the Rules

The third differential advantage strategy, called *Changing the Rules*, creates significant innovation to redefine an industry (Figure 8.8).

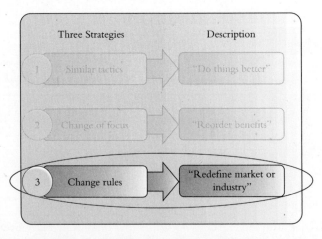

Figure 8.8 The Differential Advantage Framework: Strategy 3

As we mentioned earlier, it is critical that innovations serve an important benefit sought or value—spoken or unspoken—of your market. Many cool innovations have no market. Consider the Segway, a battery-powered electric vehicle. Although a really fast way to get around town, some people admitted that they felt stupid when they rode it.

However, the case of 1–800-Flowers shows how innovation driven by *true* unmet customer needs can change even the most mature industries.

1–800-Flowers Changes the Rules[1] Given its low-tech product—flowers—1–800-Flowers was an unlikely technology pioneer. Chief executive officer (CEO) Jim McCann purchased the rights to the ubiquitous name and number after it had floundered under previous management. He then put together a global network for delivering flowers ordered via a toll-free number to almost anywhere.

McCann recognized early the power of using the Internet to make the whole process of giving flowers and gifts quicker and more convenient. In 1992, the company launched one of the first sites on CompuServe's Electronic Mall. By 1997, a full 10 percent of the company's significant revenues were generated online—at a time when only 1.7 percent of the world's population had Internet access.

Believing correctly that online shopping was in its infancy, 1–800-Flowers sought to invest in innovations that would lock in its first-mover advantages and strengthen shopper loyalty. To find ideas that could help them achieve these goals, the company segmented its customers according to gift-giving attitudes and behaviors.

Adding a Benefit to the Well-Meaning but Overwhelmed Gift Giver Segment One main target segment for the company was dubbed the well-meaning but overwhelmed gift giver. Made up of many busy professionals, customers in this segment loved to give gifts to friends and family but often forgot important occasions due to the hectic pace of their lives.

Not surprisingly, Mary (coauthor of this book) is in this segment. Mary and her fellow segment members were very appreciative of the opportunity

---

[1]Thanks once again to our colleagues at Peppers and Rogers Group for providing background details for the 1–800-Flowers case.

to receive recommendations and assistance when transacting their gift-giving business.

1–800-Flowers realized that its significant online business gave the company a huge advantage with this segment, because the Web-based transactions made it possible to more easily capture and store key customer data than offline competitors could. Each time a member of the target segment purchased a gift online, 1–800-Flowers could store the occasion's details. This put it in a position to *add a benefit* for its online customers that its offline competitors could not easily duplicate: a remind me service.

The Calendar Club Is Born Specifically, 1–800-Flowers company offered to remind its well-meaning but overwhelmed customers when the same gift-giving occasion (birthdays, anniversaries, etc.) was about to recur. Calling the service the Calendar Club, the company received permission from members to store all relevant details of the their gift-giving transactions: date of and occasion type, recipient's name and contact information, inscription on the accompanying note, special delivery instructions, and credit card numbers used.

After initially setting up a gift-giving event through the Calendar Club, the customer would be reminded of the event when it came around again. With all the event's important details stored, the gift giver could send flowers or a gift with just a few clicks of a mouse.

Mary vividly remembers the before and after Calendar Club experience. Before being enrolled, Mary called 1–800-Flowers just two days before her mother's birthday one year. We will give Mary a break for almost forgetting; it was January 8, and she was already on a postholiday multicity trip!

Mary took care of ordering her mother's gift and was asked to join the club. The next year, on January 2, she was prompted via e-mail about her mom's upcoming birthday *and* reminded that she sent her a "lovely herb garden" the previous year. The e-mail suggested several other appropriate gifts for this year and subsequently made the entire transaction seamless by remembering the right address, credit card, and other special instructions.

Needless to say, Mary loved the entire concept immediately.

But the *real* genius of the strategy became apparent as members set up more and more occasions in the Calendar Club. Soon, 1–800-Flowers was managing a large percentage of the segment's gift-giving life. This allowed the company to retain a large percentage of the well-meaning but overwhelmed segment as competitors established an online presence, even though 1–800-Flowers was often more expensive than some other alternatives. Once these very busy customers had set up many gift-giving occasions in the Calendar Club, they were reluctant to reenter this information at another company's site to get similar service!

Mary attests to her loyalty by admitting to having "much lower price sensitivity" to 1–800-Flowers offerings due to the huge convenience it provided.

Adding a Benefit Can Lead to Significant Product Innovation, Too The 1–800-Flowers Calendar Club is a great example of applying technology to add a benefit that customers really needed, one that led to a significant service innovation that is still practical today. Companies can add significant service innovation by simply remembering things for and about customers that customers used to have to remember for themselves.

Using insights to add benefits can also lead to product innovations. Carrot sales increased when producers cut them into smaller sizes and packages for snacking, because this made carrying them around more convenient. Light beer was created by adding water to a perfectly good brew, a product innovation that added the benefit of less filling.

So now you've seen examples of all three types of Differential Advantage strategies. To summarize and provide more specifics of how to use the Differential Advantage framework and Future State Ability to Win tool to differentiate your brand, we've provided specific instructions in the tool section that follows.

POWER TOOL: DIFFERENTIAL ADVANTAGE WITH FUTURE STATE ABILITY TO WIN

USING THE DIFFERENTIAL ADVANTAGE FRAMEWORK TO BUILD A FUTURE STATE ABILITY TO WIN

To recap, the Differential Advantage framework's three strategies help you brainstorm ideas for separating yourself from competitors. The Future State Ability to Win tool can model those ideas so that you can prioritize and choose the best strategies.

(continued)

(continued)

The objective of using this chapter's framework and tool is simple: to *maximize your Ability to Win score.* As a measure of the value customers perceive your brand to be delivering in the marketplace, improving your score will translate into improved market share.

Following is practical advice for applying each step in the framework. Remember, your Current State Ability to Win analysis is the foundation for all differentiation work.

Step 1: Look for Similar Tactics Opportunities First

As discussed and illustrated in our medical diagnostics example, this is the most straightforward differential advantage strategy, so start here:

- Look at the top two or three highest-weighted benefits sought in your Current State Ability to Win and the four to six critical capabilities that go with them.
- Examine the critical capabilities that meet either of the following criteria:
  - Your company's ratings are *currently* lower than competitors', but you *could* leapfrog competitors' ratings by offering superior value with investment, focus, and execution in this area, and/or
  - *All* competitor ratings, including yours, are close to one another, and all are at or below a rating of 6; however, with some investment, *your company* could separate from the pack in this area.
- After identifying the areas that match the criteria just noted, ask yourself the following questions:
  - What would it take to improve customer perceptions in these critical capabilities and benefits sought areas?
  - Would we be able to improve enough to make a *noticeable* difference in these areas?
  - Using the highest competitor's rating in this critical capability as a benchmark, how far *could* we move our rating in improving customer perceptions with the right focus?
- Capture all potential differentiation strategies from this step for final evaluation after completing steps 2 and 3.

Step 2: Next, Look for Change of Focus Opportunities

Reordering benefits is more difficult and risky than a similar tactics approach. Nonetheless, it can be an opportunity to influence customers' thinking in a way that benefits both them and your company.

- Look at the lower-weighted benefits sought on your Current State Ability to Win.
- Examine those critical capabilities where you have a superior rating over your competitors'.
- Ask yourself the following questions:
  - Would the customer be better off placing more emphasis on the benefits sought and critical capabilities where your company has an advantage? Why?
  - Could you use strategy and strong communication to link the lower-weighted, higher-rated benefit sought to a higher-weighted benefit sought or to a value that no other competitor is serving? (For example, Nike's change of focus brought the cool factor to athletic shoes, appealing to teenager's sense of belonging—a powerful customer value.)
  - If you were successful in reorienting the customer, which benefits will they ascribe *less* weight to?
- Capture all potential differentiation strategies from this step for final evaluation. Move on to step 3.

Step 3: Now, Look for Change the Rules Opportunities

Coming up with innovation ideas is hard but important work. Many frameworks and tools have emerged for spurring marketers to think outside of the box and develop truly creative ideas.

However, we'll repeat our previous cautionary note once again: the innovations must *truly* meet customer benefits sought. Otherwise, they risk being huge wastes of time and capital.

We particularly like the innovation tools and frameworks that our business partner Bryan Mattimore developed in his book *Idea Stormers*. In fact, we've partnered with Bryan's firm Growth Engine to build a

(continued)

(*continued*)

combined innovation process that has one prerequisite: before any innovation brainstorming begins, our joint client must have a completed Ability to Win analysis.

We won't go into a deep discussion of specific innovation tools and frameworks here, but we *will* highlight one of our favorite tools from *Idea Stormers* for illustrative purposes. It's called The Worst Idea, and it goes like this:

Instead of pressuring a group to come up with some really creative ideas, the Worst Idea tool asks the group to come up with *really bad* ideas. This is a fun exercise and much less stressful than trying to imagine viable ideas right away. But there is a real purpose to the fun: we have found that the cousin of a really bad idea is a good idea.

With a little bit of thought, you can turn a bad idea into a really creative, feasible one. One of our client's terrible ideas was to send free fast-food vouchers to schizophrenia sufferers who tend to gain weight as a result of taking medicine. They turned this into a really creative, benefits-delivering initiative: creating partnerships with health food and vitamin providers to create a holistic offering with their medicine that addresses all aspects of a patient's health.

Another bad idea that an unnamed group in a high-tech industry came up with during a work session was that clients would need to take an IQ test to be allowed to purchase the product. Obviously this was absurd, but it began a discussion about how some customers understood their product, and technology in general, and how others didn't. This led to a successful segmentation approach, with the company offering different products, services, and information to each segment.

Many other innovation frameworks can be useful in helping you come up with successful product and service ideas that address customer benefits sought.

Here are the steps in developing change the rules ideas:

- Spend a good amount of time reviewing (again) the Current State Ability to Win and any other target market profile data to fix the benefits sought and values of your target market firmly in your mind.

- Next, apply innovation frameworks (such as the Worst Idea) to come up with a list of possible product and service innovations.
- Ask yourself, Which innovation ideas would most positively affect the customers' benefits sought?
- If an innovation idea does *not* match up with a benefit sought on your Current State Ability to Win, does it possibly serve an important new benefit that every competitor has missed? In other words, have you added a benefit?

Note: You must conduct research to ensure that any benefits you are adding are important to your target customers!

Capture all potential differentiation strategies from this step for final analysis.

Step 4: Model Potential Differential Advantage Strategies Using Future State Ability to Win Analysis to Ultimately Choose Your Approach(es)

The previous three steps in the process will have generated a number of ideas for differentiating your brand—more strategies than you can possibly implement. The final step is to choose those strategies that you can successfully implement and that will most positively affect your customers.

In our experience, you are more likely to succeed by investing in two or three differential advantage ideas than in spreading your resources across more areas. A small rating improvement of 1 or 2 points across a number of critical capabilities affects customers less than a significant improvement in a few important areas. It's also easier to effectively communicate a more focused strategy (but we'll discuss that more in the following chapter).

The Future State Ability to Win tool lets you calculate the change to your Current State Ability to Win score from your different differential advantage strategy ideas.

(continued)

(*continued*)

USING THE FUTURE STATE WITH SIMILAR TACTICS STRATEGIES

It's simple to use the Future State with similar tactics strategies; you just adjust your ratings scores in different areas, as done in Figure 8.9 for our medical diagnostics device marketer (repeated from earlier in the chapter).

The highlighted boxes in the ratings area show where the company believed it could move its process efficiency perception ratings (from 5 in the Current State to 9 in the Future State, and consulting from 4 to 8) with the appropriate approach. The highlighted "Total" box shows that, if successful, the company's ability to win score would move from a competitor-lagging 505 to a competitor-leading 585 score.

Benefit Sought	Benefit Weight	Critical Capability	CC Weight	Our Client Rating (1–10)	Our Client Score	Competitor A Rating (1–10)	Competitor A Score	Competitor B Rating (1–10)	Competitor B Score
New and Improved Clinical Applications	30	Better Patient Outcomes	15	7	105	7	105	6	90
		Breakthrough Apps	15	6	90	7	105	6	90
Better Imaging	25	Innovative Tech	15	6	90	7	105	6	90
		Software	10	5	50	5	50	6	60
Streamlined Operations	20	Process Efficiency	10	9	90	5	50	5	50
		Consulting	10	8	80	5	50	3	30
Funding for Research Grants	15	Link to Grant Providers	10	4	40	5	50	8	80
		Biz Case Help	5	2	10	3	15	2	10
Organizational Recognition	10	Peer Forums	5	3	15	5	25	4	20
		Media Connections	5	3	15	5	25	5	25
100			100	Total	585	Total	580	Total	545

Ability to Win Score
Increased from 505 to 585

Figure 8.9 Future State Ability to Win: Diagnostics Imaging Market

Source:

USING THE FUTURE STATE WITH CHANGE OF FOCUS STRATEGIES

Modeling a Future State Ability to Win when changing focus affects the benefit weights, making some more or less important.

This approach changes the scores of all competitors. Of course, you want to make sure your moves will actually benefit your score!

Figures 8.10 and 8.11 are the Current State and Future State Ability to Win analyses from our athletic shoe example.

The highlighted boxes in Figure 8.11 show how Nike would have modeled the opportunity to reorient customers to place more weight

Segment: Teenager Athletic Shoes		Keds		PF Flyers		Converse	
Benefit Sought	Benefit Weight	Rating (1–10)	Score	Rating (1–10)	Score	Rating (1–10)	Score
Be Comfortable	50	6	300	8	400	7	350
Find What I Need	30	8	240	6	180	9	270
Perform Better	15	5	75	7	105	5	75
Be Cool	5	5	25	5	25	5	25
	100	Total	640	Total	710	Total	720

Figure 8.10 Current State Ability to Win: Pre-1980s Athletic Shoes
Source: Copyright © 2014. Impact Planning Group. All rights reserved.

Segment: Teenager Athletic Shoes		PF Flyers		Converse		Reebok		Nike	
Benefit Sought	Benefit Weight	Rating (1–10)	Score	Rating (1–10)	Score	Rating (1–10)	Score	Rating (1–10)	Score
Be Comfortable	20	8	160	7	140	7	140	7	140
Find What I Need	20	6	120	9	180	7	140	7	140
Perform Better	30	7	210	5	150	9	270	8	240
Be Cool	30	5	150	5	150	7	210	9	270
	100	Total	640	Total	620	Total	760		790

Reorder benefits to focus on perform better and be cool

Figure 8.11 Future State Ability to Win: How Nike May Have Seen the Athletic Shoe Opportunity
Source: Copyright © 2014. Impact Planning Group. All rights reserved.

(continued)

(*continued*)

on perform better and be cool and less on be comfortable and find what I need. This allowed Nike to overtake the incumbents by reorienting teenagers to athletic shoes as a fashion item that would help them be cool.

Note that this was a streamlined example that did not include critical capabilities. In the more complete example, it would be necessary to respread the benefits weights across the critical capabilities.

USING THE FUTURE STATE WITH CHANGE THE RULES STRATEGIES

True product and service innovation, along with adding benefits, requires a little more work to model in a Future State Ability to Compete. But it is worth the effort, especially for a really big idea.

Specifically, you must determine whether adding a new benefit renders an old benefit irrelevant. Be comfortable was originally the most important sneaker benefit, but it shifted to one of the lower benefits as be cool and performance were elevated.

To keep things manageable, you might drop off the lowest-rated benefit in your Current State Ability to Compete as you model your new innovation into a Future State analysis. Then respread the weights across the critical capabilities, add in the expected ratings for yourself and your competitors, and see how the scores change.

CHOOSE YOUR STRATEGIES AND SEEK INVESTMENT

Ultimately, after modeling as many scenarios as you can, you can choose the strategy or strategies that best improve your competitive position. If you enjoy strategic thinking at all, you will have great fun with this! Finding differentiation, or viva la differentiation, is marketing's most important job and why many NonAccidental Marketers got into the field in the first place.

You will also find that the Current and Future State Ability to Win analyses will be very helpful in gaining executive buy-in and investment for your plan. Our clients often report that these analyses provide a more tangible tool and rationale for financial and executive personnel than they usually see in marketing plans. Knowing *why* marketing is asking for investment in certain capabilities and programs and what the *potential effect* will be on market share makes them more inclined to fund your initiatives!

The tools in this and previous chapters will lead you to create robust, winning strategies. The next step is to prepare to effectively communicate this strategy so that your customers will recognize the positive differences that your company brings to the market. Get ready to powerfully position your brand!

CHAPTER 9

A Positioning Statement Is a Terrible Thing to Waste

Understanding How the Mind Works to Powerfully Position Your Product

POWER TOOL: POSITIONING STATEMENT

The extra energy required to make another effort or try another approach is the secret of winning.

—Denis Waitley, American author, lecturer, and consultant

YOU OFTEN HAVE TO REJECT YOUR INITIAL CHOICE OF A POSITIONING STRATEGY

The withering stare was followed by an angry, emotional defense. "This positioning *will* work because we are the *best* at delivering on this important benefit!" The product manager was reacting to our challenge of his team's overly simplistic positioning statement, written toward the end of an intense three-day strategy workshop.

His team was working on positioning strategy, the act of choosing the image or perception a company wants to create in customers' minds. To be effective, positioning must succinctly communicate your differentiation strategy. We have good news and—as the young manager mentioned was discovering—bad news about the topic.

The good news is that all of the work you have done to this point will be extremely helpful in generating ideas for creating your positioning approach. You certainly don't want to abandon the insights that you have used to build your strategy thus far.

The bad news is that the obvious path to positioning often won't succeed. Why? Because your customers' minds operate in mysterious ways. These mysteries are being unlocked by pioneering studies into how the brain processes business-related information.

In the following chapter, we'll discuss how these findings intersect with the principles of positioning and the work you've done in previous chapters. You'll develop multiple options for your brand's positioning, which we'll illustrate through several quick-hit cases.

Often, your first choice for a positioning strategy *seems* logical and obvious. It can be frustrating to hear that it won't work, especially if you are looking to quickly finish off your marketing plan. But if you are looking to build a strategy that *radically* improves your company's sales and profits, you have to get this part right.

When you find the positioning strategy that connects perfectly with your Differential Advantage approach, you will experience tremendous success in your markets. So keep working hard; it's worth the effort.

POSITIONING DEFINITIONS

The following definitions will help you to navigate this chapter:

- *Positioning, Positioning Strategy, or Positioning Approach:* This refers to choosing the image or perception a company wants to create in customers' minds.
- *Positioning Statement:* This is a strategic document with a specific format that outlines a company's approach to creating an image or perception in the target customers' minds. A positioning statement is not the same thing as advertising copy and shouldn't be written as such. It has a much broader and strategic scope and is meant to guide all aspects of the company's value proposition/offer to its customers and stakeholders. We will provide a format for a positioning statement at the end of this chapter.

- *Positioning Promise:* This is a phrase—just a sentence or two—that succinctly embodies your positioning statement but that can also be helpful to create before developing a full positioning statement. It summarizes the unique value that customers will gain in exchange for doing business with a company. You can often use it in advertising and other marketing communications because it succinctly embodies the company's positioning.

Examples of positioning promises include statements that we will feature in the upcoming case such as most scientifically engineered brand, most trusted brand, and best combination of quality ingredients at an affordable price.

We will refer often to all three of these terms throughout this chapter.

IT'S NEVER GOOD WHEN YOU LET A COMPETITOR POSITION YOU

Positioning is a very proactive process. It has to be. If you don't choose the perception or image you want to create in your customers' minds, they will do it for you. Or worse, your competitor will be only too happy to position you.

The following example illustrates these dangers. We worked with a company that thought it had a pricing problem, when what it really had was a positioning issue, one caused by a lack of proactivity.

The company marketed nutritional food products and *thought* it was positioned in one of its top markets as the most scientific brand. However, the company's longevity in the market led customers to view the products differently—but still favorably—as traditional and trusted.

The food company, which had coasted with a dominant market share for a long time, had failed to uncover this positioning disconnect between itself and its customers. And management was very slow to react when a competitor exploited the situation by capturing the most scientific position with a new premium-priced brand. It trumpeted its product's arguably superior research and science-driven ingredients, while simultaneously lowering its price on another well-known, separately named brand. The lower-priced brand now occupied the best value position in the category. The traditional company was caught in the middle and was subtly positioned by the competitors as out of date and overpriced.

The resulting squeeze led to a difficult-to-watch free-fall decline in market share for the former market leader. The whole situation highlighted the power of positioning and the importance of doing it *proactively* based on solid principles.

THE *REAL* PURPOSE OF POSITIONING

The best positioning promises stick in customer's minds, prompting them to choose your product when you are not there to directly influence them, which, of course, *is most of the time.* Marketing plays a huge role in this, even if a company has a great sales team. You can have a very successful sales presentation, but in many cases, your customers still have to gain internal approval for the deal without you.

How will your client remember your positioning promise and powerfully articulate it in the boardroom, or make the choice you want them to make at the point of sale without you? A simple, powerful positioning promise that is designed to affix in your prospective customer's mind is the answer.

WHY YOU *MUST* UNDERSTAND A LITTLE BIT ABOUT THE BRAIN

Unfortunately, making your fundamental message memorable is not easy. Some estimates state that the average adult is now exposed to anywhere between 500 and 5, 000 marketing messages per day, and this number is only growing. Nevertheless understanding a couple of simple principles about the brain and how it remembers can give you an edge. It all starts with the concept of alpha and beta brain waves.

Beta brain waves are produced when you are doing boring and/or repetitive tasks. The body takes over and completes tasks that don't require much conscious thought. Ever finish your daily commute and realize that you don't remember the details of the drive at all? You were in a beta state.

The beta state is the brain's defense mechanism when it is overwhelmed. It is *not* the right mind state for cementing anything memorable in the mind, especially things such as positioning promises.

Conversely, *alpha brain waves* are produced when you are engaged creatively in an endeavor. Athletes, musicians, writers, artists, and other such people emit alpha waves when they are in the zone. The brain is wide open to helpful information in this state.

You can also enter the alpha state when something unusual or problematic occurs. Imagine the same boring commute mentioned earlier when, all of a sudden, a violent storm ensues. Now, with your hands tightly gripping the steering wheel at 10 and 2, you are in an alpha state, highly alert and receptive to information that will help you navigate safely.

It should be fairly obvious which state you want your prospective customers in when they hear your positioning promise so that they will remember it *and* take the actions you want them to even when you are not there.

Building a positioning promise that gets your clients' minds into an alpha state can help you ensure that they remember you in a way that positively separates your brand *when it counts.*

THE THREE PRINCIPLES OF POSITIONING TO GET YOUR CLIENT'S MIND INTO ALPHA

Product and brand positionings that embody all three of the principles in Figure 9.1 will have a high probability of putting your client's brain into an alpha state, thereby increasing your company's chances of being positioned in the way *you* want.

Each of these principles are gateways to alpha waves, but generating uniqueness is the most difficult. We'll discuss the basics of each of the three principles first and then give you some extra ammunition to ensure that your positioning is unique.

Principle 1: Importance—The Most Straightforward Positioning Strategy

Simply stated, if you don't base your positioning promise on something important to the customer, then the customer will not remember it. The evidence

- Important
- Unique
- Believable

Figure 9.1   Principles of Effective Positioning

for this is apparent in something that probably happens to you—and everyone—all the time.

Why You Can't Remember What Product That Cute Commercial You Saw Last Night Was For　Ever recall a creative, funny, or interesting commercial from your previous night's television viewing but have no idea what brand or product the ad was pushing? It's because the product itself was not *important* to you. Rest assured, if you were in the market for a new cell phone and saw an out-of-the-ordinary mobile phone commercial, you would likely remember at least the product, if not the particular brand.

Clever positioning approaches *can* nudge someone toward the alpha state; otherwise, they wouldn't be remembered at all. But if the promise is not based on something important to the customer, creative messages alone won't keep that person there long enough to make the desired impact.

This has a quite simple implication if you are following the marketing strategy process this book offers: make sure that your positioning is a *promise to deliver on the benefits sought*—or, even more powerfully, the *values* associated with those benefits—that are weighted the highest (i.e., most important to your customer) in your Future State Ability to Win analysis. Reject any approach that can't be tied back to a highly rated benefit or value.

Importance is a necessary, but not sufficient, characteristic of important positioning promises. This is where uniqueness comes in.

Principle 2: Uniqueness—Navigating the Parking Lot That Is Your Customer's Mind

Another reason for your clients' brains to reject your positioning promise is because it *lacks distinctiveness* when compared with competitors'. Positioning pioneers Al Ries and Jack Trout made many important discoveries about this principle, which they detailed in their books *Positioning* and *The 22 Immutable Laws of Marketing*.

Ries and Trout's research found that the brain likes to simplify concepts, especially when it's overloaded with stimuli. As a result, most companies' products are associated in their customers' brains with a single word or very simple concept.

For example, what comes to mind when you hear the brand name Volvo? Most people immediately think of safety/safe cars. How about McDonald's? Probably something like fast food that kids love.

Ries and Trout also found that the brain associates these concepts with *one and only one* brand or company. Thus, if you are competing with Volvo and you would like to make safety/safe cars your positioning promise, it won't be memorable.

Comparing the brain to a parking lot is a helpful analogy: if a competitor is already associated with the word or concept—in essence, that company's car is already parked in your positioning space in customers' brains—you *usually* have to find a new space.

Finding Uniqueness with a Do It Better Strategy   This brain as a parking lot analogy explains why finding a unique position is often challenging when pursuing a Do It Better differentiation approach. We learned in Chapter 8 that this strategy is about simply improving your ability to deliver on benefits sought that customers consider very important.

If *none* of your competitors are doing a good job of delivering on the benefit sought that you would like to build your position around, then this brain parking spot is open. You can seek to own a position associated with satisfying this important benefit. And as long as the benefit that you are positioning on is important to your customer, you can skip straight to the believability section of this chapter.

Unfortunately, usually at least one competitor already is positioning on the benefits sought you would like to own. If this is the case, you will have to get creative in finding a new space.

Because this happens frequently with Do It Better strategies, we have devoted an entire section at the end of this chapter to the solution, called repositioning. For now, let's cover some of the easier paths to uniqueness, starting with a Change the Focus approach.

Finding Uniqueness Is Easier with a Change the Focus Strategy   We learned in Chapter 8 that a Change the Focus strategy elevates the importance of certain benefits sought in customers' minds. Customers have undervalued these benefits in the past, so competitors have usually not already positioned themselves there. Therefore, it's likely that a competitor doesn't already own your desired positioning approach.

This makes Change the Focus positioning *strategies* straightforward when it comes to uniqueness—but not easy to *execute*. Success with this approach takes time, investment, and consistency of message to change customers' minds, so be patient.

A Values-Based Approach Can Make You Unique, Lessening the Time It Takes to Change Minds   Using values-oriented positioning will help immensely in changing customers' minds. You'll remember from Chapter 2 that appealing to *values* speaks to customers' true motivation*s*. So make sure you bring values—*emotion*—into your Change the Focus positioning promise if at all possible. Here are two examples:

1. *Nike:* We hypothesized in the previous chapter that Nike in the 1980s was focused on elevating the benefits of perform better and be cool that customers were seeking. The company's positioning and messaging from then until now have been remarkably consistent—and emotionally based. Nike's current positioning promise is values-driven: "To bring inspiration and innovation to every athlete in the world."

2. *IBM (current day):* IBM is currently positioning itself as a key business partner for companies trying to intelligently use the unprecedented amounts of data streaming into businesses these days (Big Data). Rather than appealing to the more functional aspects of helping businesses successfully deal with the data deluge, IBM is changing the focus by appealing to the emotional values of its current and potential clients. Themes of sustainability and societal progress are central to IBM's successful "Smarter Planet" campaign.

Finding Uniqueness with a Change the Rules Strategy   Change the Rules strategies present the one opportunity to take on established competitors head to head in positioning on benefits and/or values that they already own. This is because you are bringing a *significant* innovation to your market or industry. In this situation, the positioning challenge becomes one of powerfully articulating how your innovation *uniquely* delivers.

A great approach for helping you figure out your unique Change the Rules promise comes, once again, from our innovation business partner, Bryan Mattimore, and his book *Idea Stormers*.

It's called the billboard technique, and it works like this: marketers imagine that members of their target market drive by a prominent billboard at highway speed every day on their way to work.

After studying the benefits sought and values that their innovation addresses, the team creates a single sentence or phrase that summarizes the product's positioning in benefits-oriented language and posts that on the billboard. The resulting positioning promise helps the marketers communicate the benefits of their innovation in customer-friendly terms.

We use this technique to generate positioning promises for marketers pursuing a Change the Rules type of strategy. Past famous billboards provide great examples and thought starters for this approach.

The iPod's original billboard ads were meant to communicate the huge innovation that the mp3 digital music format brought to a world where Sony's Walkman ruled. The innovation was so huge that Apple stuck with a more functional, yet undeniably powerful, positioning: "10,000 songs in your pocket."

Federal Express's hub-and-spoke air fleet management strategy brought significant innovation to the overnight package delivery service many years ago. FedEx's early positioning went with a more emotional, risk-avoidance promise targeted at its business-to-business customers: "When it absolutely, positively has to be there overnight."

The billboard technique also helps reinforce the positioning principle of importance, focusing an innovative Change the Rules positioning promise on what really matters to customers.

Use of the Importance and Uniqueness Principles Helps Shift Your Prospects' Brain Waves into Alpha Waves What is really happening as you use the principles of importance and uniqueness is that the customer's brain is working consciously *and* subconsciously to evaluate your positioning. Done correctly, your positioning will move the customer's brain into an alpha state. You have the person's attention, which is hugely important.

At this point, most customers want to validate whatever subconscious or emotional processes have been triggered in their minds. This is where the third principle of believability comes into play.

Principle 3: Believability—The Rational Mind Takes Over

The believability principle simply requires you to cite significant evidence to support your important and unique positioning promise. Your marketing and sales communications provide you with the opportunity to develop believability.

The best advice is to assume that your customer base is a jury and that you are presenting evidence to support your positioning claim. Your approach depends on your overall strategy.

Believability in Do It Better strategies requires lots of supporting points, or one very compelling argument, because you are not bringing a new idea or major innovation to the market. One of our clients was introducing a new consumer lawn fertilizer against a major, entrenched competitor. The team found something compelling to support their promise of "a lawn that is the envy of your neighbors."

The product was targeted at Lawn Enthusiasts, people who took care of their own lawns and cared *only* about the grass, to the exclusion of other landscaping elements. The compelling, *believable* support point of their positioning promise? The product was already used by a large percentage of the biggest Lawn Enthusiasts ever: 80 percent of U.S. golf course superintendents in the United States!

Believability in Change the Focus strategies requires consistency and a strong connection to something that the customer currently cares about. Nike linked its fashion-oriented benefits to a sense of belonging in teenagers. A review of its advertisements over time reveals a clear consistency of message as well.

Developing believability in Change the Rules strategies is straightforward, as long as you can back up your positioning with a demonstration or guarantee. When Apple introduced the iPod, no other device could put 10,000 songs in your pocket. Demonstrations in Apple stores was all the evidence that was required. FedEx's "absolutely, positively" claim was backed up by guarantees that stood behind the promise to get packages delivered overnight.

POSITIONING ELEPHANTS IN A LARGE INDUSTRIAL COMPANY

A few years ago, we were working with a large industrial plastics company (which we will call Big Plastic Co.) that had been buying up smaller companies. As the company's chief executive officer (CEO) reviewed some disappointing sales results with his executive team, he began to sense that the company had a positioning problem.

"I'm not sure what we stand for in our customers' minds," he said after hearing of big variations in outcomes with key accounts. We were asked to help this company discover how they were positioned.

We conducted several interviews with both large existing accounts and potential customers. After starting with some conventional research questions, we began to elicit some insight by asking the following: "Sometimes characteristics of an animal are similar to that of a company. What type of an animal best resembles Big Plastic Co.?"

Following some initial laughter, they consistently answered that Big Plastic Co. was "like an elephant." Probing deeper, we found out that "they have large ears, but they don't listen to us" and "they get going in one direction and don't change."

We asked the customers how this affected their relationship with Big Plastic Co. The typical answer was something like, "Oh, we don't give any of our new prototypes to Big Plastic Co.; we give them to the smaller, more flexible companies."

Big Plastic's CEO was so angry that his company was positioned as an elephant that he issued the Stun Gun Award. This award would be given to anyone in the organization that was able to help change the company's positioning from an elephant to some more desirable image, like a cheetah.

One production manager found that he could shift production runs and dedicate a line to prototypes. The resulting Flexible Prototype Program became very successful. Today, the company continues moving away from its elephant position to proactively creating a more positive image in the minds of its customers.

What type of an animal do you think that your customers would say your company or product resembles? More important, why would they think that? What animal would you prefer to resemble? If you don't like the answer, what can you do to reposition?

REPOSITIONING: THE SOLUTION TO DIFFICULT POSITIONING PROBLEMS

So what do you do when a competitor already owns your desired position? This often happens when pursuing a do it better strategy. In fact, this was the case with the angry manager we mentioned at the opening of this chapter.

His team wanted to position on a benefit that a competitor was known for. They were committed to focusing on and investing in a benefit area to make their company's offering the best.

We had no doubt that they would eventually exceed their competitor's ability to win in this area. But it was not a situation in which they could *radically* improve on the competitor's offer. The competitor was also investing pretty heavily in satisfying the benefit.

As we explained to the manager, you can't simply shout competitors out of a positioning space they already own. Our customers' brains don't work that way. The solution to this struggle comes from an approach that we call *repositioning*.

Repositioning is the process of finding a unique angle for your company when the benefit you want to own is already taken. Done correctly, it updates or establishes your position to a desirable space and often downgrades your competitor's image in your customers' minds. If you think about the Ability to Win from the previous chapter, the competitor's ratings may drop, or the benefits that that competitor owns would start to have a lower weight in customers' minds.

REPOSITIONING APPROACHES

Here are three prospective repositioning approaches:

1. *Values-Based Repositioning:* Sometimes competitors own a functional benefit sought in customers' mind but have not created a values-oriented positioning. This gives you an opportunity to develop a unique, values-focused position that is more motivating to and powerful to customers. This approach also effectively repositions competitors as more mundane. We've seen two examples of this already, both from Chapter 2, plus another popular example of this approach:
    *   *Skin cream:* Olay climbed to number 1 in the U.S. market by creating a values-oriented positioning promise of be young/youthful looking when others were focused on a more functionally oriented promise of soft skin.
    *   *Holiday Inn Express:* Holiday Inn Express won over the price-conscious business traveler with a values-oriented positioning promise of "Stay Smart" when others were focused on the more functional promise of low price.

- *MasterCard:* MasterCard has made big inroads in Visa's market share, helped by its emotional positioning promise of "priceless." The addition of this values-oriented message—"some things money can't buy, for everything else there's MasterCard"—seems to be effectively one-upping Visa's more functional "accepted everywhere" message.

2. *The "Opposite-Good" Repositioning Strategy:* When a competitor owns a powerful position in your customers' minds, you may be able to find an *opposite* position that is still beneficial to the customer—and, again, can cast the competitor in a more negative light. For instance, the good opposite of biggest can be fast/nimble; the good opposite of fastest could be highest quality; and so on. Here are some famous examples of the opposite-good strategy, the latter two of which were mentioned in previous chapters:

   - *Avis:* The famous "We are #2 so we have to try harder" promise positioned the company as hard-working. The approach took significant market share from the leader, Hertz, casting Hertz in a big and complacent light.

   - *IBM from the 1960s to 1980s:* Although their positioning promise of "No one ever got fired for buying IBM" was unofficial, you can bet that IBM sales conversations at the time trumpeted this message. The positioning had maximum impact because it appealed to IBM customers' values of risk avoidance, while positioning new, more innovative technologies as risky.

   - *Listerine:* Also from Chapter 2, Listerine repositioned Scope's tastes good positioning with "the taste you hate, twice a day," leveraging customers' natural inclination to think that a strong taste equaled strong medicine.

   It's possible that this approach might cause you to invest in additional or new Differential Advantage strategies. Avis had to develop operational practices that proved that it was "trying harder" than Hertz in giving customers what they wanted.

3. *The Subdivision Repositioning Strategy:* Ries and Trout found that customers easily remember the *first* person, brand, or company to create a new category. For example, everyone remembers Charles Lindbergh as the *first pilot* to traverse the Atlantic via airplane. And everyone remembers Amelia Earhart's name because she was the *first woman* to do so. But does anyone remember that Bert Hinkler also did it—in between Lindbergh and Earhart?

Repositioning via subdivision *creates* a new category that you can be first in. You can use this strategy when you feel you *must* position your company on a benefit or value that a competitor already owns. You subdivide your category so that you can claim to be the first or *only* brand to focus on a particular industry or segment. Consider the following examples, the first two from earlier chapters:

- *Dell:* Not the first to sell computers, but the first to sell computers *directly to customers* for personal and business use.
- *Enterprise:* Not the first to sell rental cars, but the first to focus on the home market (versus traveler) segment.
- *Amstel Light:* Not the first light beer in America, but the first *imported* light beer.

Did your earlier work on the Influence Map (Chapter 1) uncover new stakeholders or a new route to market, like Dell? Did your work in Chapters 3 and 7 uncover new segments that you can be the first to target like Enterprise? If so, the subdivision approach might work well for you.

PUTTING IT ALL TOGETHER

In summary, your approach to positioning is strongly dependent on your strategy for differentiating. You *must* position on something that truly matters to customers (importance) and find a position that honors the way customers' brains work (uniqueness, using repositioning if necessary). Finally, it's imperative that you find evidence that strongly supports your desired position (believability).

To wrap up the topic of positioning, let's look at how you can bring all this chapter's information together.

TOOLS: POSITIONING STATEMENT—A FRAMEWORK TO HELP YOU POSITION

Here are the steps to develop an important, unique, and believable positioning statement and promise:

STEP 1: DETERMINE THE POSITIVE POSITION ALREADY OWNED BY YOUR COMPETITORS

Examine one or two of the competitors from your Ability to Win analyses. What is the word or phrase that they already own for your target customers?

For ideas, look at the benefits sought from your own Ability to Win analysis. Often, your competitors are already associated with benefits upon which you want to build positioning. Acknowledge this tough fact if it is true, and avoid the temptation to associate them with something negative; they must be doing *something* right, or they wouldn't have any business at all.

Write down these competitor positions. They are the existing perceptions that you must position against.

STEP 2: DETERMINE THE *IMPORTANT* BENEFIT SOUGHT OR VALUE THAT YOU WANT TO OWN IN THE MINDS OF YOUR CUSTOMERS

If a competitor does not already own this benefit, you have an important *and* unique benefit and can move onto step 4, believability. However, if you want to position on a benefit that a competitor already owns—or if you are bringing a significant new innovation to market—move on to step 3.

But before you move on, examine the values associated with the benefit you want to own using the WIIFM technique from Chapter 2 or consult your benefits ladder. Write down the benefit/value you want to own and move on to the next step.

STEP 3: STRENGTHEN THE UNIQUENESS OF THE BENEFIT SOUGHT OR VALUE THAT YOU WOULD LIKE TO OWN

To find or strengthen your uniqueness, try the repositioning approaches of *Values-Based, Opposite-Good* and *Subdivision* from earlier in the chapter. Write down the new benefit or value that you would like to own

(continued)

(continued)

in your customers' minds. Rework your Future State Ability to Win if necessary.

If you are bringing a significant new innovation to market, use the Billboard Technique from earlier in this chapter. The output of this technique is likely the positioning promise for your strategy.

A tip for checking the uniqueness is to scratch out your product or company name in your positioning and write in a competitor's name. If the positioning is still true, your statement isn't unique enough.

STEP 4: GATHER THE BELIEVABILITY EVIDENCE FOR YOUR POSITIONING

Brainstorm and write down existing and new evidence that you will produce to support the ownership of the desired benefit sought or value. However, don't despair if you need more ideas; the upcoming value proposition chapter will provide more.

For **Change the Focus** strategies, write down how you will elevate the importance of the benefit sought or value you wish to own— and how you will link it to a benefit or value that is *currently* viewed as important by your customers.

For Change the Rules strategies, write down how you will *demonstrate* the believability of the positioning promise you developed in the previous step using the Billboard Technique.

STEP 5: CREATE A POSITIONING STATEMENT

A positioning statement is a strategic document that outlines your approach to a market. It guides all aspects of the company's value proposition/offer to its customers and stakeholders.

Creating a positioning statement is *much easier* when you have completed the previous 4 steps. Now, all that is necessary is to capture your work in the document, massage it so it makes sense, and move on to step 6. Figure 9.2 is a positioning statement outline, with instructions for how to create it with the elements of your strategy that you've already developed.

Elements	Positioning Statement Formula
Target Stakeholder or Segment	
Customers' Core Needs (to demonstrate importance)	
Our Offering Name	
Competitive Frame of Reference	
Point of Difference (what will we uniquely provide)	
Our Support (so that our offer is believable)	

Figure 9.2   Sample Positioning Statement

Source: Copyright © 2014. Impact Planning Group. All rights reserved.

Elements	Positioning Statement Formula
Target Stakeholder or Segment	To deep-sea oil drillers working in extreme and isolated conditions
Customers' Core Needs (to demonstrate importance)	Who need to maximize the productivity of offshore assets and mitigate the financial impact of unscheduled downtime
Our Offering Name	Offshore drillers fast response service
Competitive Frame of Reference	Oil and gas industry service packages
Point of Difference (what will we uniquely provide)	Is the only offering in the industry that includes immediate response benefits while eliminating typical industry features that deep-sea drillers don't need
Our Support (so that our offer is believable)	Featuring less than 24-hour reponse through flying service engineers to your rig, while reducing the need for idle maintenance resouces to put more control in your budget

Figure 9.3   Sample Completed Positioning Statement

It's helpful to look at a completed example. Figure 9.3 is a full positioning statement for a business-to-business company. We will provide more details on this company's strategy in Chapter 10.

(continued)

(*continued*)

After creating your company's positioning statement, review it carefully. Is it important, unique, and believable? If yes, move onto the final step.

STEP 6: CREATE A POSITIONING PROMISE

The positioning promise is a pithy version of your positioning statement. It embodies the essence of the image you want to create in customers' minds. If you haven't created the promise already, you can use the Billboard Technique described earlier in this chapter to create it.

For the example we just highlighted, the oil and gas services company could boil its positioning statement down to the following powerful promise:

Service engineers to your deep-sea rig in less than 24 hours.

Through positioning, your overall marketing strategy is starting to come to life. You are now ready to conclude your strategy at the place where many less enlightened marketers *start* their marketing strategy process—working on the 4 Ps of value propositions. Prepare to finish strong as we move on to the final chapter of this book!

CHAPTER 10

Reinventing a Commodity

How Starbucks Is Able to Fetch $2.75 for an 8-Ounce Latte

POWER TOOLS: VALUE PROPOSITION IDEA CATCHER AND PERCEIVED VALUE ANALYSIS (PVA)

However many holy words you speak, what good will they do if you do not act upon them.

—Buddha, sage and founder of Buddhism

WORKING ON THE 4 Ps COMES AT THE *END* OF THE STRATEGIC MARKETING PROCESS

A lot of participants get anxious during our multiday workshops. They want to know: "When are we going to talk about the 4 Ps?"

Until they are exposed to strategic marketing tools and processes, many believe that marketing's job is *only* about figuring out 4 P plans: product, place, promotion, and price (to which many nowadays add a fifth P for people). Some marketers are pigeonholed into focusing *exclusively* on promotions and marketing communications pieces.

But we have a much broader view of marketing's role, which you hopefully share after reading this far. Marketers should be the *orchestrators* of the entire organization's strategy. It's their job to bring together information about the market, customers, and their own company's capabilities. As such, building a

4 P value proposition is the *last step* in a sound strategic marketing process. It's not a company silo where marketers live.

Our process has given you a clear focus on your target market's needs, a differentiation strategy that will separate you from competitors, and a positioning approach that will stick in customers' minds.

Now, it's time to shape all of this into a brilliant 4 P strategy—but not like you've done before. This final chapter will open your mind up to new 4 P strategies that you likely would have missed had you not worked on approaches such as Needs-Based Segmentation and Ability to Win. You'll find new ideas for designing your product, getting it to your target market, and making the most out of your promotional budget.

Pricing is especially crucial. There is no bigger sin in business than undermining your strategy by leaving money on the table—*or* getting overly greedy when it comes to price. Fortunately, there is a very simple yet powerful tool that builds off of your Ability to Win work that allows you to set an optimized pricing strategy. Whether your goal is to be value-priced, premium-priced, or something else, the pricing tool will help you maximize profit margins.

So get ready to bring all of your work together to cover the 4 Ps, and we'll end the book by answering a popular inquiry: "How can Starbucks thrive when it charges so much for a cup of coffee?"

AS YOU CREATE YOUR VALUE PROPOSITION: AVOID THE LUKEWARM TEA SYNDROME!

Remember Chapter 3's story about medical diagnostics marketer Quidel's highly successful segmentation? Although the core pregnancy test product was the same for both of its target segments, *almost everything* else about the value proposition varied. We've reprinted one of the charts from that chapter in Figure 10.1.

When applying frameworks and tools to create a value proposition, you must design each 4 P component with your target segment's needs in mind. And if you are targeting more than one segment, consider strongly the opportunity to create *separate* value propositions for each segment.

This will keep you from watering down your value proposition to something that averages different customer segments' needs—and will help you avoid the temptation to make the dreaded lukewarm tea discussed in Chapter 3.

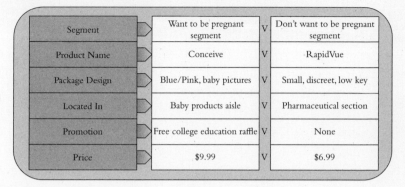

Figure 10.1 Quidel's Customized Value Proposition

Source: Rita Koselka, "Hope and Fear as Marketing Tools," *Forbes*, August 29, 1994.

THE VALUE PROPOSITION IDEA CATCHER

Accidental Marketers who create value propositions need idea-generating tools and frameworks and a place to capture the best strategies. We call the framework shown in Figure 10.2 the Value Proposition idea catcher, which will also be useful in guiding us through each of the four parts of this chapter: product, place, promotion, and price.

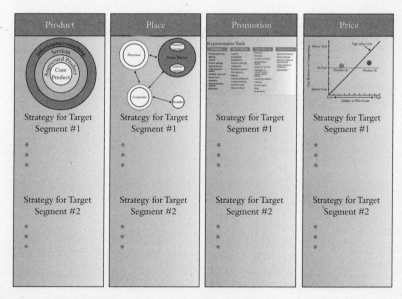

Figure 10.2 The Value Proposition Idea Catcher

Source: Copyright © 2014. Impact Planning Group. All rights reserved.

THE FIRST P: REDESIGNING YOUR PRODUCT OFFER USING THE BULL'S-EYE

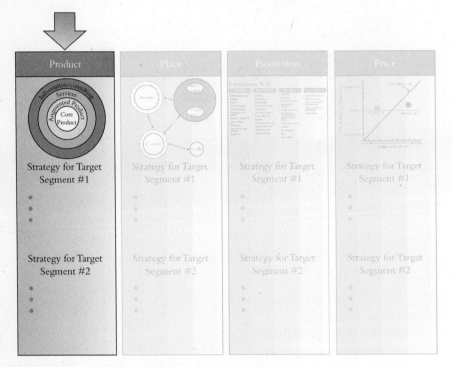

Figure 10.3   Product Section of the Idea Catcher

So how—and where—do you get ideas for redesigning your product to better meet your target market's needs? By considering the framework of "the whole product," an idea that marketing professor Theodore Leavitt first introduced.

We've modified Leavitt's original model somewhat to something we call the bull's-eye framework. Each rung comes with an accompanying question that prompts you to think broadly about several aspects of your product, while keeping your target market in mind (Figure 10.4).

Let's go through each rung and accompanying question, with examples to illustrate:

- *Core Products:* By looking at your target customer's benefits sought and values, you can begin to explore ways to alter your actual, physical product (or core service) in ways that they will appreciate. Even industries with significant regulatory hurdles that make new product variations

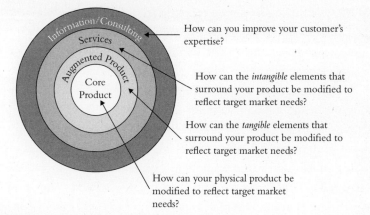

Figure 10.4   The Bull's-Eye Framework for Product Value Propositions

challenging are doing this. For example, many pharmaceutical companies are creating longer-lasting, extended-release versions of their medicines for on-the-go customers seeking efficiencies in their lives.

Infant nutrition manufacturers are creating different brands for different segments—no lukewarm tea here. Formulations with expensive ingredients are marketed as premium brands, and formulas with standard ingredients are targeted toward the less affluent value-minded mom.

If your core product is a service, you can configure your core service in different ways that reflect segment needs—and create products around your service. A client that provides services to companies drilling for oil and gas offers to fly service engineers via helicopter to the site within 24 hours for its high-risk deep-water segment. Other segments required less speed and thus a lower-priced, different service configuration.

- *Augmented Product:* Packaging, copromoted products, and special instructions all qualify as tangible elements that surround your product, the subject of the augmented product ring on the bull's-eye framework.

    Packaging, in particular, is a popular source of customized value proposition ideas because it is often easier to modify for different segments than actual physical products. Look at Quidel's segment-specific packaging strategy for evidence of this principle in the consumer products world.

    For a business-to-business (B2B) example, consider how Netherlands food distributor SPAR augments its product in a highly customized way.

SPAR will pack groceries on pallets in any configuration specified for its high-volume grocery store clients. Most stores request that they pallet the groceries to match their stores' layouts, which saves them valuable time in the stocking process.

Starbucks had to adjust its original augmented product value proposition. In the fabulous account of Starbucks history called *Pour Your Heart into It,* Howard Schultz discusses how he and the early management team thought that to-go cups were heresy and that espresso drinks tasted much better in ceramic cups. But this didn't suit the needs of its original target market of urban coffee lovers who were always in a hurry. The ubiquitous Starbucks paper cup and holder was a concession to target market needs that ended up being a walking advertisement for the company.

Even the most modern of products need augmentation. The stock prices of Facebook and LinkedIn have been on fire as of this writing. Both of these social media platform companies have developed applications that are optimized for use on mobile phones. No matter how big your company is, how old it is, or how well (you think) you're doing, you must always examine the tangible elements that surround your product—and see if you can alter them to reflect your target segment(s) needs.

• *Services:* Another important component of your whole product offering are intangible elements that are not part of the physical product or packaging. These service components include warranties, maintenance agreements, and support agreements for situations that arise in the use of a physical product. For instance, a client that sells sophisticated manufacturing machinery can remotely monitor the machines it sells for an additional fee. This monitoring allows the company to predict when its client's machines are going to break down before they do, saving clients from costly downtime. The company can leverage the client's usage data to provide advice on optimizing the machine's productivity.

For companies whose core product is a service, the service ring on the bull's-eye should say "products." In other words, service providers "productize" offerings in this layer. Our own company provides a service: marketing strategy consulting. This book is a productized version of our services offering. So is our cloud-based marketing toolkit, which offers electronic versions of the frameworks and tools in this book to our clients.

- *Information and Consulting:* In a world exploding with information, customers appreciate any help they can get in filtering out noise and obtaining solid, unbiased advice. The "information" part of the information and consulting ring can help a company figure out how to be one of these filtering agents that customers value so much these days.

Specifically, knowing a segment's needs and providing information—usually at no charge—to make them more knowledgeable about your product *category* positions a company as an industry expert. You can see many B2B executives and marketers on LinkedIn positioning themselves and their companies in just this way.

Above, we discussed how one of our B2B clients collected information about the usage patterns and performance of its equipment at its client's site. To make its value proposition more robust with information, the company provided a customized maintenance schedule that was tailored to its client's workflow.

Providing information to consumer product buyers via a website is common as well. And the smartest marketers use segment-specific information to make *different* information available for different segments. It's pretty easy to come up with these informational variations if you have strong segmentation. Amazon learns the ways that you seek and purchase products and is great at serving up recommendations specific to your needs (e.g., wish lists, discounts).

Try it yourself with the examples we've provided. What types of information and consulting might you provide in a Quidel pregnancy test kit for the want to be pregnant Conceive product purchasers (e.g., tips on designing a nursery, getting pregnant, juggling work and children)? And how might this differ for the don't want to be pregnant RapidVue product purchasers (e.g., advice on avoiding pregnancy, adoption services, managing as a single parent)?

The "consulting" part of the information and consulting ring usually involves delivering more detailed advice for a fee. B2B technology and software product vendors often offer consulting services to customers. Companies that purchase Cvent software use the product to help them streamline and optimize event planning, something most firms typically spend 1 to 3 percent of their annual budget on. Of course, the software only speeds up failure *if you have bad processes* in the first place. Cvent offers event planning consulting services that help companies take advantage of the company's domain expertise. The consulting generates a significant amount of the company's revenue.

• *Naming Your Whole Product Offer:* Giving different core offerings distinct names can be powerful when altering these products or services. It worked well for Quidel's Conceive and RapidVue products (see also Chapter 3), as well as for the oil and gas services provider mentioned earlier.

Having differently named offerings for different segments communicates the message that you have *designed something specifically* for the customer. It also helps align your thinking around other value proposition elements that you can tailor for the segment.

THE SECOND P—PLACE—STRATEGY IS LARGELY DRIVEN BY YOUR INFLUENCE MAP

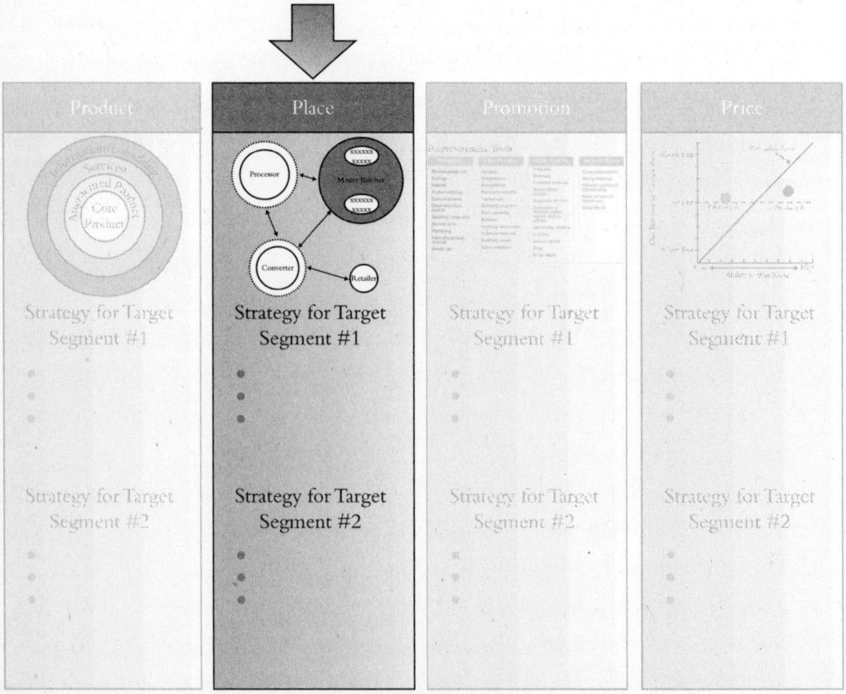

Figure 10.5   Place Section of the Idea Catcher

Place strategy is about *where* you will sell your product—and *who* will sell it. You want to look to your influence map for ideas on this.

The emergence of a new stakeholder can change *where* you sell enormously. Just ask Dell. You'll recall from Chapter 1 that the growing trend of self-reliant consumers shifted the *place* of personal computer sales from retail to direct-to-home sales.

Less radical but important place strategies often spring up from examining B2B influencer maps—as our medical manufacturer of artificial replacement hips, also from Chapter 1, found out. Calling on hospital administrators, who cared more about the longer surgery time required than the hip's technically superior features, was an unchartered place that the company had missed in the past.

Utilizing place strategy often uncovers an influencer that a brand hasn't focused on in the past. A company may have to develop new organizational skills to effectively reach these influencers—and hire new personnel with the necessary experience.

Many specialty drug manufacturers—which make products that treat rare disorders—are finding huge changes in their influence maps. For many years, they have been able to place almost all their resources against selling to specialist doctors. But that's no longer the case. Nowadays, patients and caretakers can educate themselves online about these diseases and options. As a result, they often come to their specialist doctor with a strong preference for specific treatment. Many of our clients in this field have had to shift resources away from their professional sales forces to fund the hiring of Web strategists who can develop online patient communities.

THE THIRD P—PROMOTION— COMMUNICATES YOUR POSITIONING TO YOUR TARGET MARKET AND HIGH-PRIORITY STAKEHOLDERS

Promotional strategy is the high-level plan for the primary channels you will use to communicate your positioning to your target market and key stakeholders. There are so many methods for promoting a product that often our clients are overwhelmed when it comes to developing this strategy.

Although this portion of the value proposition is often highly visible in consumer-type products such as cars, hotels, and home furnishings, it is just as important in B2B situations.

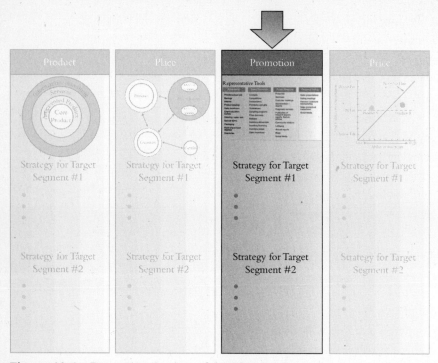

Figure 10.6   Promotion Section of the Idea Catcher

A great way to get the discussion started is to decide which past promotional tactics, events, and messages that you will *stop* now that you have a deeper understanding of your target market and their needs. Companies tend to be creatures of habit: by looking at which are no longer advisable based on your overall strategy, you can then start to free up mind space—and budget—for new approaches.

One pharmaceutical company found that generalist physicians were not referring a high percentage of patients with a particular disorder to a specialist. The physicians lacked the skills to diagnose the rare disease, leaving many patients untreated. So the company shifted their promotional strategy, which had been largely oriented toward specialist conferences and meetings, to allocate some budget to create diagnosis tools for general physicians. They also began attending the conferences that these generalists frequented.

The result was a substantial uptick in referrals to specialists. Patients were treated earlier, and the company benefited from a proportionate share of the new prescriptions being written.

Positioning promises can drive very creative promotional ideas. Lexus's promise in the United States is "status and service." Promotions—such as the one we discussed in Chapter 6 where the company offers free parking to Lexus owners at sporting venues in well-placed lots—are driven by this promise.

Often, it helps to bring in domain experts to help drive promotional strategy. With our partner Response Marketing, we help clients go from zero to a complete set of strategically driven creative promotional concepts in five days through our Rapid Evolution (REV) approach.

Response Marketing's chief executive officer (CEO), Carolyn Walker, believes—and we agree—that the secret to effective promotion is to have a tight strategic marketing approach *before* generating creative promotional concepts. As Carolyn points out, "Promotional creativity means nothing if it doesn't help the top and bottom lines. Our team is *always* creative, but when we can create ideas guided by a well-thought-out differentiated strategy, we can literally do magic!"

The bottom line with promotional strategy: don't let creative promotional tactics—or the promotions you've done in the past—be the tail that wags the dog. Use your target market and key stakeholder needs, as well as your differential advantage strategy and your positioning promise, as a guide when choosing where and how you will spend your promotional budget. *Then* get creative, whether with the help of an agency or on your own.

Figure 10.7 is a list of the many different tactics you can use to drive your promotional strategy. Note that some of the more popular ones are social media and blogs (depending on the market), although the traditional methods such as sampling and customer meetings are still highly effective.

THE FOURTH P—PRICE—IS A FUNCTION OF YOUR ABILITY TO WIN AND YOUR PRICING GOALS

There are many ways to cut costs in a business, but it is estimated that a 1 percent improvement in price results in an average of an 11 percent increase in profits. With this kind of leverage, it's no wonder that many resources, including the article by Michael Marn and Robert Rosiello titled "Managing Price, Gaining Profit," cite pricing as everyone's favorite topic of the 4 Ps.

Advertising

Print/broadcast ads
Mailings
Internet
Product catalogs
Sales brochures
Client education leaflets
Detailing/sales aids
Service items
Packaging
Point-of-purchase displays
Directories

Sales Promotion

Contests
Competitions
Sweepstakes
Premiums and gifts
Tradeshows
Sampling programs
Price discounts
Rebates
Inventory allowances
Inventory financing
Inventory swaps
Sales incentives

Public Relations

Press kits
Seminars
Customer meetings
Sponsorships/awards
Diagnostic services
Publication of research papers, reports, feature articles
Community relations
Lobbying
Annual reports
Blogs
Social Media

Personal Selling

Sales presentations
Selling meetings
Inbound/outbound telemarketing
Sales contacts at tradeshows
Social Media

Figure 10.7   The Promotional Mix: Representative Tools

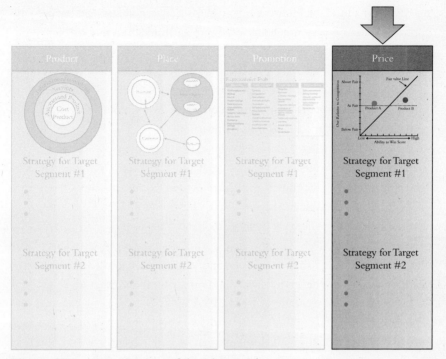

Figure 10.8   Price Section of the Idea Catcher

However, companies struggle mightily to establish a pricing strategy and set effective prices. We observe that there are basically three types of pricing approaches, which we call the three Cs.

The first C stands for the cost-based method. Using this approach, price is set at some predetermined percentage markup over costs.

The second C method stands for the competitor-based method. This approach fixes prices at some percentage above or below the price of a competitor's product.

Despite the wide usage of both the cost-based and competitor-based methods, both of these pricing tactics have major flaws.

For one thing, you're leaving money on the table in instances where you *could* charge more than a cost or competitor-based approach suggests. And if you have no idea how customers value your product, you could end up with a price that makes no sense to them.

The way to fix this is to employ the third C, called the customer value-based method. This approach sets prices according to the *value* customers receive from a product. However, many pricing strategists struggle to apply this approach, because they don't know how to quantify the value of their products or services.

The good news for Accidental Marketers is that the Ability to Win tool is exactly what is needed to set customer value-based prices. The score from this approach quantitatively measures customers' perceptions of the value of a company's offering and those of its competitors.

By cross-referencing Ability to Win scores against prices charged in the marketplace, value-based pricing strategies indeed become possible. The tool that puts price and customer perceptual scores (Ability to Win) together is called the Perceived Value Analysis (PVA). Our friend Bradley Gale, in his popular book *Managing Customer Value,* introduced it to us.

According to Bradley, "Companies use PVA as a customer-focused, fact-based approach for earning market share gains and/or price premiums." Our clients love the approach because it flows logically and simply from our other tools.

Figure 10.9 is an example of what a PVA looks like.

In the PVA in Figure 10.9, contractors perceive product A (assume a pink soft insulation product installed in commercial buildings) to have an Ability to Win score of roughly 800. The insulation manufacturer is charging a price that is slightly above average for the market they compete in, or slightly above par.

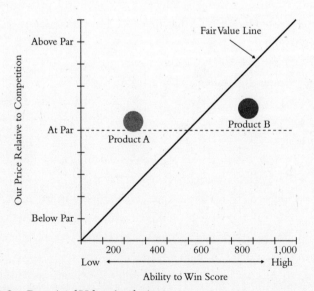

Figure 10.9   Perceived Value Analysis

Product A (assume a white, more scratchy insulation product) is perceived to have an Ability to Win score of around 300 by contractors, of which its manufacturer is charging a price that is about average in the industry.

The fair value line, running diagonally across the chart and intersecting par at an Ability to Win score of 500, shows what most customers would view as a fair price at various levels of value. Simply stated, a company delivering an average amount of value—a score of 500—should charge a price that is around average for the industry. And as companies add more or less value to their offering, they can alter the price accordingly.

Customers in this example perceive product A as delivering less than average value while charging an average price, which puts them above the Fair Value line. Product A loses sales because of this.

Product B, however, is perceived as delivering significantly more value than product A at a price that is only slightly above average. This puts them below the Fair Value line, meaning that customers perceive them to be delivering very good value for the price. Product B is maximizing its sales volumes because its pricing *makes sense to customers.*

No matter where your current position is on a PVA, you can adjust price, improve your Ability to Win score, or both in optimizing your pricing strategy. See Figure 10.10 for a deeper dive into this concept.

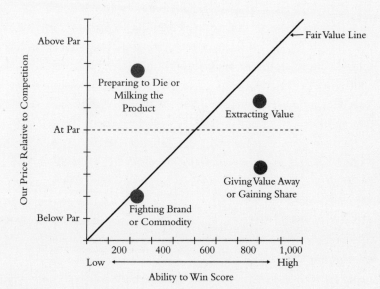

Figure 10.10   Analyzing the Perceived Value Chart

- *Upper left PVA quadrant:* The upper left PVA quadrant shows where product A (the white scratchy insulation) was in the original example. Companies that find themselves here are about to lose significant market share. They either have to lower their price, improve the value they deliver, or do both. However, companies will often intentionally price in this quadrant to milk profits from a mature product that will soon be off the market. This may be a good short-term pricing strategy, depending on your situation.

  Many of our global B2B clients are in this quadrant when they first enter third-world markets. Their U.S.-based research and development (R&D) groups engineer sophisticated equipment that companies with basic needs don't yet need—and therefore don't value. The in-country marketers are forced to figure out how to rectify the situation and often lose share to local companies with a more basic value proposition and a lower price.

- *Upper right PVA quadrant:* A plot anywhere in the upper right-hand quadrant means that a company is extracting fair value. Pricing near the fair value line while giving above average value typically optimizes sales and profits for a brand.

- *Lower right PVA quadrant:* The lower right hand quadrant is the home of a pricing strategy that is leaving money on the table. This is likely a scenario where customers would pay more for your product because you are delivering high levels of value (i. e., high Ability To Win score). One technical services client of ours realized from its PVA that it was not charging enough for its conferences—which were chock-full of events and valuable information that competitors didn't offer. The company raised its conference pricing by a factor of 33 percent, while still selling all available seats. This dropped an additional $400,000 immediately to the company's bottom line.

  One company that made a snack product targeted at children used a PVA to evaluate its planned introductory price in a huge developing market. It plotted the product in the lower right quadrant. The company subsequently raised the introductory price by the equivalent of 5 cents and still met its initial sales projections. In a country of more than 200 million children, this had the effect of creating a significant amount of additional profit.

- *Lower left PVA quadrant:* This is where fighting brands or commodities—those that intentionally offer limited value and charge an equivalently low price—live. As the fair value line in this quadrant suggests, customers know when they are making a value-price trade-off.

Many of the global marketers we mentioned use the fighting brand strategy in emerging markets after their initial struggles selling overengineered, over-priced products. They take away all of the product and service extras that the emerging market customer wants, which allows the company to charge less.

Of course, this strategy can dilute an upscale brand's positioning promise. But there is an easy answer to this dilemma. *Change the name* of the fighting brand to something else. Make it clear to customers what they are getting. Don't confuse them by having a value offering and a premium offering under the same brand.

This was the problem we saw with Volkswagen from Chapter 6, where the VW badge on the Phaeton confused potential customers. A company that seemed to get this right is Marriott Hotels, where Fairfield Inn provides a much different experience than their JW Marriott brand . . . or even their company-owned, high-end Ritz-Carlton hotels.

THE FINAL STORY OF THE BOOK: STARBUCKS BALANCES THE PRICE VALUE EQUATION TO REINVENT A COMMODITY

The PVA helps answer a question we get from Accidental Marketers all the time: "How does Starbucks get away with charging so much more than its competitors for a cup of coffee?" We'll end this chapter with an interesting PVA analysis that explains this phenomenon.

When Starbucks was in its start-up phase, most Americans had not yet been introduced to dark-roasted coffees. Americans mostly drank *Robusta,* a type of coffee widely believed to be inferior to richer, darker *Arabica* blends. Howard Schultz—originally the marketing vice president for Starbucks when it was a coffee bean retailer and now its chairman and CEO—wanted to bring these richer coffees to U.S. consumers' consciousness.

But Schultz wanted Starbucks to do much more than simply provide a core product of a superior cup of coffee. He was also captivated by something else he saw on a business trip to Milan, Italy: he noticed that the espresso bars in Italy served an *emotional* purpose that went beyond a simple caffeine jump-start to the Italian workday. In Italy, the coffee shop was a place of community and escape from the normal.

Looking beyond the fact that most Americans had yet to be introduced to espressos, lattes, and cappuccino, Schultz set his sights on recreating this atmosphere with a total value proposition.

Before—and After—Starbucks, Most Convenience Store Coffee Costs about a Buck

Before Starbucks came along, people typically purchased their morning coffee at a place like a 7-Eleven convenience store, for around $1.00. The as-yet unrefined American coffee drinker had simple needs around this experience: convenience, consistency, and taste. Many thought this would never change. In fact, some European and American would-be investors in Starbucks passed up the opportunity.

Europeans didn't think Americans could slow down enough to appreciate the finer points of the premium coffee experience. Others assumed that Americans couldn't possibly embrace such a big change in what was then a commodity market.

Surely those who passed on the opportunity to get in on the ground floor of Starbucks are mystified by the chain's success. But not you! Armed with the tools in this book, you can unlock such mysteries of marketing success.

Starting with a re-creation of the pre-Starbucks target segment's needs, we can look at a pre-Starbucks Current State Ability to Win, a post-Starbucks Ability to Win, and a PVA to see how they did it (Figure 10.11).

Segment: Urban Morning Coffee Drinkers				Convenience Store		Fast Food Drive-Thru	
Benefit Sought	Benefit Weight	Critical Capability	CC Weight	Rating (1-10)	Score	Rating (1-10)	Score
Convenience	50	Well Located	30	7	210	6	180
		Fast Service	20	5	100	7	140
Consistency	25	Hot	15	7	105	7	105
		Fresh	10	5	50	5	50
Taste	25	Medium Strength	15	5	75	5	75
		Selection of Styles	10	5	50	5	50
	100		100	Total	590	Total	600

Figure 10.11 Ability to Win Analysis: Pre-Starbucks

Based on our interviews with pre–Starbucks era coffee drinkers, the most important benefit sought from the cup of morning joe was convenience. Being able to get their "jump-start in a cup" without having to awaken (or "wake up") any earlier in the morning or risk arriving to work late was paramount.

Convenience stores and drive-thrus fulfilled this convenience need the best, and there were negligible differences between the two. Preference for one or the other was likely driven by whether your commute was via public transit (e.g., convenience stores near train stations or work) or by car (e.g., a drive-thru on the way).

The other two important benefits were a reflection of the less refined coffee palate Americans had at the time. There was wide tolerance and a low bar when it came to consistency and taste. The important things were that the cup of coffee was reasonably hot and fresh, was not too strong, and included the availability of decaffeinated coffee for those trying to manage their intake.

As we see from the total Ability to Win scores, both types of providers were doing a reasonable job of delivering on modest expectations. And with a per cup price of around $1.00, the whole price value equation made reasonable sense to most consumers, as the PVA in Figure 10.12 shows.

Now let's look at the Starbucks value proposition, particularly the product bull's-eye (Figure 10.13). Starbucks introduced many new factors to coffee lovers in their recreation of the Italian espresso bar experience.

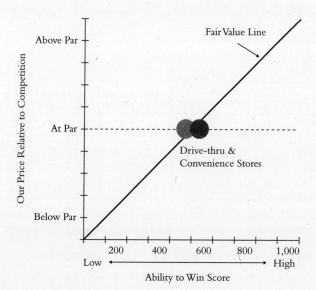

Figure 10.12   Perceived Value Analysis: Pre-Starbucks

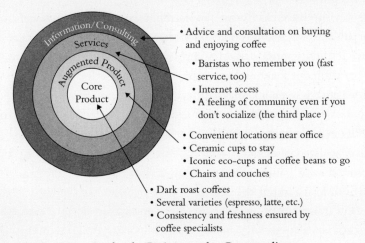

• Advice and consultation on buying
and enjoying coffee

• Baristas who remember you (fast
service, too)
• Internet access
• A feeling of community even if you
don't socialize (the third place)

• Convenient locations near office
• Ceramic cups to stay
• Iconic eco-cups and coffee beans to go
• Chairs and couches

• Dark roast coffees
• Several varieties (espresso, latte, etc.)
• Consistency and freshness ensured by
coffee specialists

Figure 10.13   How Starbucks Reinvented a Commodity

Starbucks' full offer not only generated a new perception about its own company with coffee drinkers but also reset expectations and perceptions about existing coffee retailers. In Ability to Win terms, Starbucks did some things better, reordered some benefits, and changed some of the industry's rules.

Not only did its execution of this strategy establish a high Ability to Win score for Starbucks, but it also lowered competitors' perceptual scores. Let's look at a sample Ability to Win after Starbucks, shown in Figure 10.14.

Segment: Urban Morning Coffee Drinkers				Convenience Store		Fast Food Drive-Thru		Starbucks	
Benefit Sought	Benefit Weight	Critical Capability	CC Weight	Rating (1-10)	Score	Rating (1-10)	Score	Rating (1-10)	Score
Convenience	30	Well Located	20	6	120	5	100	8	160
		Fast Service	10	5	50	7	70	7	70
Consistency	20	Hot	10	5	50	5	50	9	90
		Fresh	10	4	40	4	40	9	90
Taste	30	Quality Beans	15	3	45	3	45	9	135
		Selection of Styles	15	4	60	4	60	9	135
Experience	20	Place to Work	10	1	10	1	10	8	80
		Place to Socialize	10	3	30	1	10	8	80
	100		100	Total	405	Total	385	Total	840

Figure 10.14   Ability to Win Analysis: After Starbucks
Source: Copyright © 2014. Impact Planning Group. All rights reserved.

Specifically, Starbucks likely reduced the importance of the benefit sought of consistency, not because hot and fresh coffee became less important, but because it became *table stakes*. Because Starbucks coffee was always hot and fresh, it heightened awareness of the times where the convenience stores and drive-thrus served lukewarm, stale coffee.

Specifically, this would have downgraded the perceptions customers had about the existing competitors; you can compare the ratings from the before-and-after analyses to see this.

Starbucks also raised the bar on the benefit sought of taste. People started wondering about the quality of beans convenience stores and restaurants were using. Often, these places came up lacking when compared with Starbucks.

The newcomer also opened people's minds to what selection in coffee really meant. Simply providing decaf as an alternative was no longer going to cut it—not with tongues that had tasted espresso, lattes, and cappuccino at Starbucks. Again, perceptual ratings likely declined for the incumbents.

Convenience remains an important benefit sought today, and Starbucks' ambitious location strategy showed that it recognized this. Although convenience shows a lower benefit sought weight in our post-Starbucks ability to win, it's only because Starbucks introduced a new benefit: the coffee experience.

Coffee was a social drink in America long before Starbucks. The company just created a new, more appropriate place for it to be enjoyed.

This phenomenon has often been referred to by Schultz as the third place. No one was going to rush you out of a Starbucks if you wanted to stay. It was a place where it was okay to hang out that wasn't home, wasn't work, and wasn't a bar!

Interestingly, Starbucks research uncovered the fact that even people who didn't say a word to others while they were there considered it a place for positive social interaction. And the introduction of free Wi-Fi made it a great alternative place to do work.

This had the effect of adding the benefit sought of experience to the coffee-drinking equation. Convenience stores and drive-thrus couldn't compete here either. The resulting Ability to Win shows the enormous difference in value to the experience that Starbucks brought. And as we've seen with the PVA analysis, enormous differences in value justify enormous differences in

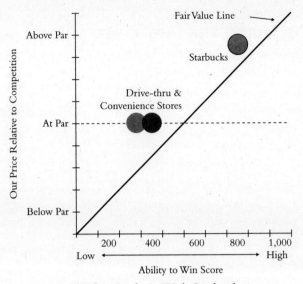

Figure 10.15   Perceived Value Analysis: With Starbucks

price to the customer. The post-Starbucks PVA shown in Figure 10.15 puts the situation into perspective.

The analysis shows that drive-thru and convenience store prices have largely remained at par, while the perception of their coffee has been diminished, even as many have upgraded their beans and varieties somewhat. In comparison to Starbucks, many think of these alternatives as swill!

And although Starbucks appears to be on the high side of the fair value line, the enormous difference in value over the previous alternatives justifies the price gap. We hear many people complain about Starbucks' high prices, but their sales continue to grow.

Starbucks shows what is possible when you design a full strategy that reflects an understanding of target market needs, a differentiated value proposition, and pricing that makes sense to customers. Especially if you are in a business that is often thought of as a commodity, this case shows how you can use the tools in this book to reinvent yourself and bring new value to a mature industry.

TOOLS: USING THE PERCEIVED VALUE ANALYSIS TO MANAGE PRICE

The value proposition idea catcher at the beginning of the chapter is a great framework for communicating your 4 P strategy—and how your approach will differ for different segments. In addition, the PVA can provide some very powerful workings. The final part of this equation is where we will close this chapter: on the topic of managing price.

Marketers tend to love the PVA; however, they are not sure how it translates into the type of daily pricing situations that occur, especially in B2B scenarios. How can a PVA help companies selling technical products in competitive industries manage price better?

In our experience, just the *process of building* a PVA is helpful to salespeople in negotiations. The Ability to Win, Differential Advantage, and positioning exercises help laser in on the reasons that a company's value proposition is superior, in ways that really matter to customers.

Many of our clients use the PVA plot as a strong reference point for pricing negotiations. They find that they can adjust pricing up or down based on the actual and future client potential.

In all cases, companies that use a PVA tell us that they are able to manage price better overall; the analysis gives them the courage and confidence to stick to their guns better in negotiations. And those that cannot justify their current pricing know exactly how to improve their Ability to Win scores and value proposition in optimizing their sales and profits.

Closing Remarks

Congratulations! Now that you have journeyed through the 10 critical marketing topics presented in the book, you may be feeling a bit more like an on-purpose marketer, or even a passionate marketer, than an accidental one.

We hope that as a result of reading this book, you are more empowered in creating your own strategy and marketing plans. Likely, *The Accidental Marketer* helped you realize that marketing strategy is more scientific and rational than you thought. That's what working with tools and frameworks can do: help you make sense out of brilliant strategies that previously seemed to be random acts of genius.

BRINGING *ART* INTO YOUR DISCIPLINED, TOOLS-DRIVEN APPROACH

It's important to know that there *is* still a significant artistic side to strategy. The *art* of marketing comes into play as you operate more and more imaginatively *within The Accidental Marketer* tools and frameworks.

For instance, significant right-brain thinking is valuable when it comes to building a Benefits Ladder (Chapter 2), brainstorming Dimensions of Segmentation (Chapter 3), developing Change of Focus or Change the Rules differentiating strategies (Chapter 8), and creating unique Positioning Statements and Value Propositions (Chapters 9 and 10). As with many disciplines, consistent use of *The Accidental Marketer* tools will bring a proficiency that encourages your creativity further. Clients who have fully integrated our approach prove this to us all the time; their level of differentiation and business results just keeps getting better and better.

Another area that requires artistic thinking is in the interplay *between The Accidental Marketer* tools. Often, you will uncover an idea—say, in your positioning work—that leads you to revisit your segmentation. A willingness to look at your plan as fluid until it is the best it can be is a good habit to get into—and an important key to success.

ORCHESTRATING YOUR COMPANY'S STRATEGY

In addition to your strategic proficiency, we hope that you also have gained the confidence to now guide a cross-functional team of your colleagues to work through the tools to obtain fresh insights from different perspectives.

Marketers are perfectly positioned to be the orchestrators of a company's strategy. Who else can bring together the perfect mix of market, customer, competitor, and company resources and insights to facilitate a powerful plan that the entire organization supports?

We can promise you that the tools and frameworks we've outlined in this book make the challenge of coordinating cross-functional inputs into a successful marketing strategy much easier. We know, because this is the type of work that we do every week with companies all over the world.

ADDITIONAL RESOURCES FOR ACCIDENTAL MARKETERS

Even as your confidence and proficiency as a marketer grow, you will encounter challenges not covered in this book. We have therefore made more resources available to you at our website: www. theaccidentalmarketer.com.

There you will find:

- *Assessment tool and book shortcut:* If you are in a hurry and want a fast answer to your marketing challenge, our short assessment will highlight the most relevant chapters in the book to address your issue.
- *Information about our automated toolkit:* Our cloud-based electronic toolkit features automated versions of most of the frameworks covered in the book. It can save you time in developing your marketing plan.

- *An opportunity to interact with us and other Accidental (and Experienced) Marketers:* share your success stories, questions, and viewpoints on the world of marketing. You can interact with other marketers and get in touch with us if you'd like direct help in solving your marketing-related challenges.

We will be adding even more resources to this site over time.

Thank You and Best Wishes on Your Marketing Journey!

In closing, we'd like to express our appreciation to you for reading this book. Fueled by our clients' challenges, we gain constant motivation to search for new answers to the question, "What drives marketing success?"

Although we believe we've begun to unlock some of the secrets to marketing greatness, we know that much work is left to be done. Like all great topics, there is always another layer to explore.

To us, the entire quest of discovery is a journey to be enjoyed. We truly love our work and embrace the continuous process of digging deeper still. And we are thrilled that a whole new set of Accidental Marketers like you will join the discussion after reading this book.

We wish you the very best of success on your marketing journey.

Tom Spitale and Mary Abbazia

Resources

CHAPTER 1: WHO MOVED MY. . . . CUSTOMER

The following sources were referenced as we reverse-engineered the history of Dell Inc.'s reshaping of the personal computer market.

1. Michael Dell and Catherine Fredman, *Direct from Dell: Strategies That Revolutionized an Industry.* New York, NY: HarperBusiness, 1999.
2. Statistics about the growth rate of PC usage between 1980 and 1985 came from Database, World Development Indicators. "Personal Computers Statistics," Nation Master, accessed October 11, 2013, NationMaster.com.
3. Information on SolarWinds was, in part, gathered from Marilyn Alva, "SolarWinds Scores Big Growth on the Little Tech Guys," *Investors Business Daily,* August 10, 2012.
4. SolarWinds quarterly earnings and sales growth figures were obtained from MarketSmith (www.marketsmith.com), an online subscription service, on December 21, 2013.
5. Dell's website reports that the company became "the No. 1 computer systems provider worldwide" in 2001: "Our History," Dell, accessed on October 11, 2013, www.dell.com/learn/us/en/uscorp1/our-history.

CHAPTER 2: THE FOUNTAIN FROM WHICH GREAT MARKETING FLOWS

The information for this chapter's many snippets and stories came from the following:

1. The automobile commercial reference in the beginning of the chapter is referring to a 2012 Hyundai Sonata advertisement.
2. We have had the great pleasure of working with Dr. Michel Tuan Pham and his highly successful Executive Education program at Columbia.
3. Many classic ads can be found at www.youtube.com, including the Apple "Think Different" campaign.
4. The Olay banner ad displayed in the chapter appeared during a Google search for "skin cream" on June 14, 2013.
5. The Listerine story was sourced from several informative sources, including the following site that chronicles history of Johnson & Johnson: "LISTERINE® Antiseptic: A Very Useful Product." Kilmer House, accessed October 12, 2013, http://www.kilmerhouse.com/2008/02/listerine-antiseptic-a-very-useful-product/.
6. Paxil's approach to depression in Japan was sourced from a *New York Times* article on August 22, 2004, and was supplemented by our friend and client, Jason Humphries, marketing director at GSK and General Manager at Bristol-Myers Squibb.
7. Entering "Listerine Ads of the 1920s" into a Google search will yield a plethora of ads like the ones we reference in the chapter.
8. The announcement of the FTC's refutation of Listerine's claims of fighting colds and sore throats was found at: "Cold? Sore Throat? Listerine Won't Help." *The Evening Independent* [St. Petersburg, Florida], December 9, 1974, A: 3.
9. One of the "Hang in There" Listerine commercials can be found at YouTube: http://www.youtube.com/watch?v=P1mlJPb1l6s.
10. The Barnes and Noble story was sourced, in part, from the following: "Look Into Customer's Souls," *Forbes Managing,* March 7, 1994.
11. Some of the details of the launch of the Holiday Inn Express brand came from: "IHG® Launches First Integrated Campaign for Holiday Inn Express in UK & Germany," Hospitality Net, accessed October 12, 2013, http://www.hospitalitynet.org/news/4062338.html.
12. Information about the market research driving Holiday Inn Express and the brand's history was sourced from: Stephen P. Smith, *America's Greatest Brands, Volume 5: An Insight into Many of America's Strongest and Most Trusted Brands.* New York: America's Greatest Brands, 2006.
13. Many of the great "Stay Smart" commercials can be viewed at http://www.youtube.com/results?search_query=holiday+inn+express+stay+smart&oq=holiday+inn+

express+stay&gs_l=youtube. 1. 0. 0l2. 4809. 9686. 0. 11669. 28. 16. 2. 10. 10. 0. 112 . 1043. 15j1. 16. 0. . . 0. 0. . . 1ac. 1. 11. youtube. LEdEpwK1vGU.

CHAPTER 3: ARE YOU MAKING LUKEWARM TEA?

1. In addition to the references that follow, the Quidel story was developed through an October 8, 2013, interview with Bob Gergen, currently vice president of sales for Rapid Pathogen Screening, Inc., and a former member of the Quidel marketing team. Many thanks to Bob for his insights!
2. Rita Koselka, "Hope and Fear as Marketing Tools," *Forbes*, August 29, 1994.
3. John Forsyth, Sunil Gupta, Sudeep Haldar, Anil Kaul, and Keith Kettle, "A Segmentation You Can Act On," *McKinsey Quarterly*, no. 3, 1999.
4. A good definition of Occam's razor is at http://www.merriam-webster.com/ dictionary/occam's razor.
5. Larry Selden and Geoffrey Colvin, *Angel Customers & Demon Customers: Discover Which Is Which and Turbo-charge Your Stock*. New York: Portfolio, 2003.

CHAPTER 4: WHAT BUSINESS ARE YOU *REALLY* IN?

The details of Southwest's interesting and successful history were referenced from the following sources:

1. Kevin Freiberg and Jackie Freiberg, *Nuts! Southwest Airlines' Crazy Recipe for Business and Personal Success*. Austin, TX: Bard, 1996.
2. "Our History—Southwest Airlines Newsroom." Southwest Airlines Newsroom, accessed October 12, 2013, www.swamedia.com/channels/Our-History/pages/ our-history-sort-by.

The contrasting story of People Express came from the following sources:

3. "History of People Express," *Aviation Online Magazine*, accessed October 12, 2013, http://avstop.com/history/historyofairlines/peoplexpress.htm.
4. Eric Kochneff, "The Rise and Fall of PEOPLExpress," Airliners.net, August 13, 2004.

The Jack Welch quote in the chapter came from:

5. Jack Welch and Suzy Welch, *Winning.* New York: HarperBusiness, 2005.

Other items from the chapter:

6. "Metabolomx, Diagnosing Disease by Breath Metabolic Signature," Metabolomx, accessed October 12, 2013, http://metabolomx.com.
7. "A Breath of Cancerous Air," *Business Week,* March 2012.

CHAPTER 5: WHO DO YOU LOVE?

The story of Enterprise was put together from the following sources:

1. "Auto Rental News," Auto Rental News, accessed October 14, 2013, www.auto rentalnews.com.
2. Kirk Kazanjian, *Exceeding Customer Expectations: What Enterprise, America's #1 Car Rental Company, Can Teach You about Creating Lifetime Customers.* New York: Currency Doubleday, 2007.
3. "When Is It Time to Pivot? 8 Startups on How They Knew They Had to Change," ReadWrite, accessed October 19, 2013, http://readwrite.com/2012/10/18/when-is-it-time-to-pivot-8-startups-on-how-they-knew-they-had-to-change.
4. Sarah Bartlett, "Seat of the Pants," Inc.com, accessed October 14, 2013, www.inc .com/magazine/20021015/24772.html.
5. "Local Market Revenue Grows Past Airport," *Auto Rental News,* January 2006.
6. There is a lot written about the service recovery paradox; some believe it works only in certain instances. You can enter the term in your browser and get plenty of scholarly discussions about the phenomena.
7. "Enterprise Rent-A-Car Company History," History of Enterprise Rent-A-Car Company—Funding Universe, accessed October 14, 2013, www.fundinguniverse .com/company-histories/enterprise-rent-a-car-company-history/.
8. "Enterprise Rent-A-Car Career Site," Enterprise Rent-A-Car Careers, accessed October 14, 2013, www.erac.com.
9. Special thanks to longtime colleague Tom Niehaus (Niehaus Enterprises, LLC, Tom@NiehausEnterprises.com) for providing the case on the AIDS drug at the end of this chapter.

CHAPTER 6: WHAT *WERE* THEY SMOKING?

The background information on the Phaeton was gathered from the following:

1. Jack Ewing, "Mercedes-Benz A-Class: Trading Upright for Swept Back," *New York Times,* October 14, 2013.
2. "Biggest Automotive Missteps: Volkswagen Phaeton," CarBuzz, July 22, 2012, http://www.carbuzz.com/news/2012/7/22/Biggest-Automotive-Missteps-Volkswagen-Phaeton-7709839/.
3. Al Ries, "Ad Age Blogs & Columnists," Advertising Age Al Ries RSS, December 5, 2005, http://adage.com/article/al-ries/volkswagen-phaeton-failed-u-s-market/47646/.
4. "Dr. Piëch's Legacy: Hits and Misses from a Distinguished Career," *Car and Driver,* February 2011.
5. Ryan Konko, "Why the Volkswagen Phaeton Failed in the U.S.," The Car Connection, August 14, 2009, http://www.thecarconnection.com/news/1034260_why-the-volkswagen-phaeton-failed-in-the-u-s.
6. "2007 Volkswagen Phaeton," Top Speed, accessed October 14, 2013, www.topspeed.com/cars/volkswagen/2007-volkswagen-phaeton-ar1309.html.
7. Peter Robinson, "Volkswagen Phaeton 4MOTION W-12," Car and Driver, September 2002, http://www.caranddriver.com/reviews/volkswagen-phaeton-4motion-w-12-first-drive-review.
8. Erik Ayapana, "Thread of the Day: Which Cars Are Over-Engineered?" Motor Trend, May 9, 2012, http://wot.motortrend.com/thread-of-the-day-which-cars-are-over-engineered-203593.html.
9. Gabe Nelson, "VW Phaeton Will Return to the U.S." Automotive News, July 22, 2013, http://www.autonews.com/article/20130722/OEM03/307229970/#.
10. Jake Holmes, "We Hear: Volkswagen Phaeton Rejoining U.S. Lineup?" Motor Trend, July 17, 2013, http://wot.motortrend.com/we-hear-volkswagen-phaeton-rejoining-u-s-lineup-386591.html.

The story of Lexus was developed using the following sources:

11. Chester Dawson, *Lexus: The Relentless Pursuit.* Singapore: Wiley, 2004.
12. Brian Long, *Lexus: The Challenge to Create the Finest Automobile.* Dorchester: Veloce, 2000.
13. "Everything about LEXUS," LEXUS Models & Brand History, AutoEvolution, accessed October 14, 2013, http://www.autoevolution.com/lexus/.
14. John P. Huffman, "1978 to 1983 Audi 5000," Popular Mechanics, accessed October 14, 2013, www.popularmechanics.com/cars/news/industry/4345725–4#slide-4.

Chapter 7: The Magnetic Effect of Focus

Michael Porter's quote about the essence of strategy has been seen in numerous sources, including the following:

1. Michael E. Porter, "How Competitive Forces Shape Strategy," *Harvard Business Review,* 1979.

The Magnetic Mind-Set chart was adapted from the following seminal work from Peppers and Rogers:

2. Don Peppers and Martha Rogers, *The One to One Future: Building Relationships One Customer at a Time.* New York: Currency Doubleday, 1993.

Facts about the Iridium case were referenced from:

3. Sydney Finkelstein and Shade H. Sanford, "Learning from Corporate Mistakes, The Rise and Fall of Iridium," *Organizational Dynamics,* 29: 138–148.
4. Lynette Luna, "Iridium's Resurrection," Connected Planet, January 22, 2001, http://connectedplanetonline.com/mag/telecom_iridiums_resurrection/.
5. "Iridium," Satellite, M2M Connectivity, accessed October 14, 2013, www.m2mconnectivity.com.au/technologies/satellite/iridium.
6. "Iridium Surpasses 500,000 Subscribers Worldwide," Iridium Communications Inc., Iridium, September 12, 2011, http://investor.iridium.com/releasedetail.cfm?ReleaseID=604474.
7. "Overview," Iridium, accessed October 14, http://www.ex4u.org/Iridium_Overview.php.

Information for the BlackBerry case was sourced through:

8. The information on BlackBerry's stock price was sourced from www.marketsmith.com, a subscription service, on October 9, 2013.
9. Elizabeth Woyke, "A Brief History of the BlackBerry," *Forbes Magazine,* August 17, 2009, http://www.forbes.com/2009/08/17/rim-apple-sweeny-intelligent-technology-blackberry.html.
10. Clayton M. Christensen, *The Innovator's Dilemma: When New Technologies Cause Great Firms to Fail.* Boston, MA: Harvard Business School, 1997.
11. Clayton M. Christensen, Scott D. Anthony, Gerald Berstell, and Denise Nitterhouse. "Finding the Right Job For Your Product," *MIT Sloan Management Review,* Spring, 2007.

Sources of information about Apple:

12. Quarterly sales figures were sourced from www.marketsmith.com, on October 9, 2013.

13. Walter Isaacson, *Steve Jobs*. New York: Simon & Schuster, 2011.

CHAPTER 8: VIVA LA DIFFERENTIATION

1. We gained a new perspective on our business from Virginia (Ginny) Ertl at GJ ConsultingWorks: ginny.ertl@gmail.com.

Resources for the Nike story were the following:

2. For information on the process and considerations for buying sneakers in the 1970s, we interviewed our parents!

3. "History & Heritage," NIKE, Inc., accessed October 15, 2013, http://nikeinc.com/pages/history-heritage.

4. "History of Nike," KicksOnFirecom, Sneakerhead.com, accessed October 15, 2013.

5. Stephen M. Pribut and Douglas H. Richie, "2002: A Sneaker Odyssey," *APMA News,* July/August, 2002.

6. Kenneth Labich and Tim Carvell, "Nike vs. Reebok a Battle for Hearts, Minds & Feet," *Forbes,* September 18, 1995.

7. Jack McCallum, *Dream Team: How Michael, Magic, Larry, Charles, and the Greatest Team of All Time Conquered the World and Changed the Game of Basketball Forever.* New York: Ballantine, 2012.

8. Martha Sherrill Dailey, "Jordans in 1985 and Now: A Frenzy Afoot." *Washington Post,* December 23, 2011, http://www.washingtonpost.com/blogs/arts-post/post/jordans-in-1985-and-now-a-frenzy-afoot/2011/12/23/gIQAQbgsDP_blog.html.

In addition to the details provided by a Peppers and Rogers Group case study, further details for the 1–800-Flowers story were sourced at the following:

9. "1–800-FLOWERS, Inc. History," Funding Universe, accessed October 22, 2013, http://www.fundinguniverse.com/company-histories/1–800-flowers-inc-history/.

Special thanks to our business partner, Bryan Mattimore, for the ideas referenced in the chapter from his book, reference follows. This is a must-read!

10. Bryan W. Mattimore, *Idea Stormers: How to Lead and Inspire Creative Breakthroughs.* San Francisco: Jossey-Bass, 2012.

CHAPTER 9: A POSITIONING STATEMENT IS A TERRIBLE THING TO WASTE

Information on alpha and beta brain wave states was sourced from:

1. Keith Brown, *Excellence Option*. FriesenPress, 2013. Victoria, BC, Canada.

We also referenced two of our favorite classic marketing books in this chapter:

2. Al Ries and Jack Trout, *Positioning: The Battle for Your Mind*. New York: McGraw-Hill, 1986.
3. Al Ries and Jack Trout, *The 22 Immutable Laws of Marketing: Violate Them at Your Own Risk*. New York, NY: HarperBusiness, 1993.

Others references from this chapter:

This will take you to some of the great commercials from MasterCard's "Priceless" campaign:

4. "Brett Favre MasterCard Priceless," YouTube, May 18, 2007, http://www.youtube .com/watch?v−ZoEGYFzS0jA.

A great account of the Avis "#2" story is available at:

5. "The Sell! Sell! Blog: Advertising Greatness #2: Avis," sellsellblog.blogspot.com, accessed October 15, 2013, http://sellsellblog.blogspot.com/2008/09/advertising-greatness-2-avis.html.

More information on IBM's "Smarter Planet" campaign can be found at:

6. "An Introduction to IBM's Smarter Planet," YouTube, February 1, 2011, http:// www.youtube.com/watch?v=QZ0o7avcvv4.

You can get a look at some of the original iPod billboards at the following site:

7. "The Pop History Dig » IPod Billboard Ads," www.pophistorydig.com, accessed October 15, 2013, http://www.pophistorydig.com/?tag=ipod-billboard-ads.

Here's where you can see some classic FedEx commercials from the "absolutely, positively" era:

8. "Baer Performance Marketing—Green Bay, WI," www.baerpm.com, accessed October 15, 2013, http://www.baerpm.com/blog/?p=264.

CHAPTER 10: REINVENTING A COMMODITY

If you missed it in Chapter 3, the Quidel value proposition was sourced from:

1. Rita Koselka, "Hope and Fear as Marketing Tools," *Forbes,* August 29, 1994.

The following references Theodore Levitt's introduction of the "whole product" concept:

2. Theodore Levitt, "Marketing Success through Differentiation—of Anything," *Harvard Business Review,* January 1980.

The following two references have details about SPAR and ORTEC's pallet customization processes:

3. http://www.ortec.com/~/media/Files/Infortec_Articles/English/Infortec_global_2009_ttl_spar.pdf.
4. http://www.ortec.com/us/Solution/Pallet_and_Load_Building.aspx.

The statistics about leveraging price to gain profit was from the following source:

5. Michael V. Marn and Robert L. Rosiello, "Managing Price, Gaining Profit," *Harvard Business Review,* September 18, 1992.

Special thanks to Bradley Gale for his perceived value analysis (PVA) tool, first introduced in:

6. Bradley T. Gale and Robert Chapman Wood, *Managing Customer Value: Creating Quality and Service That Customers Can See.* New York: Free, 1994.

The following were sourced for the details of the Starbucks story:

7. Howard Schultz and Dori Jones Yang, *Pour Your Heart into It: How Starbucks Built a Company One Cup at a Time.* New York, NY: Hyperion, 1997.
8. Our informal research of pre-Starbucks coffee drinkers was conducted in July and August 2013.

Index